CLOTHES TO SEW FOR 11½" Fashion Dolls

Volume 1

LINDA WRIGHT

To Genevieve, my first fashion doll

Also by Linda Wright

Credits
Photography: Linda and Randy Wright

All rights reserved. No part of this book may be reproduced, stored in a retrieval system, or transmitted, in any form or by any means, electronic, mechanical, photocopying, recording, or otherwise, without prior written permission from the publisher. Permission is granted to photocopy patterns and templates for the personal use of the retail purchaser.

Copyright © 2024 Linda Wright
Edition 1.4

Lindaloo Enterprises
Santa Barbara, California
United States

ISBN: 978-1-937564-18-6
Library of Congress Control Number: 2024907481

CONTENTS

INTRODUCTION 6
Fashion Doll Measurements 6
Fabric 7
Tips & Tools 7
General Directions 8

GARMENT GALLERY and SEWING INSTRUCTIONS

Flower Power Dress 11
Shift Dress 13
Straight Skirt, Bandeau & Fingerless Gloves 15
Spaghetti Strap Swing Dress 17
Overshirt, T-Shirt & Mock-Drawstring Shorts 19
Princess Dress 21
Wrap Coat & Trapezoid Purse 23
Peplum Blouse & Leggings 23
Christmas Tree Set 27
Straight-Leg Jeans & Flared Top 29
Sock Sheath Dress 31
Runway Dress 33
Skirted Bikini & Beach Towel 35
Palazzo Pants & Ruffle Blouse 37
Yoke Skirt, ¾ Sleeve Top & Hat 39
Ruched Top & 3-Tier Skirt 41
Swing Cardigan 42
Denim Jacket 43
Pom Pom Dress 45
Maxi-Skirt & Crop Camisole 47
Starshine Jumpsuit & Spats 49

Simple Dress 51
Babydoll Dress 53
Nightgown 55
Bathrobe 55
Hosiery 56
   Tights 56
   Thigh-High Stockings 57
   Socks 57
Apron 58

FULL-SIZE PATTERNS 59

ABOUT THE AUTHOR 125

INTRODUCTION

This collection of patterns includes more than 40 garments and accessories for 11½" Fashion Dolls. You will find casual wear, fancywear, playwear, swimwear, sleepwear, legwear, outerwear and holiday wear. Besides dresses, there are separates that you can mix-and-match to create myriad outfits.

This is a doll clothes pattern book. As such, it requires an understanding of sewing basics. General directions and helpful tips are included on the next few introductory pages — and additional hints are sprinkled throughout the book.

If you are new to sewing, or unfamiliar with certain techniques, YouTube.com offers a wide assortment of excellent video tutorials. Beginners can watch the fundamentals of pinning and cutting pattern pieces, machine sewing, and hand sewing. Demos of specific methods and products are plentiful, such as how to gather fabric; sew darts; make pleats; turn narrow tubes right-side out; use a loop turner; sew on buttons and snaps; apply fusible tape; or alter a pattern. I have assembled a collection of my favorite educational sewing videos on Pinterest. You can view them at www.pinterest.com/LindalooEnt/ on a board named "Sewing Basics".

The standard seam allowance for these patterns is 1/4" (6mm). It is very important to be accurate since even a tiny variation can throw off the fit of such small clothing. A 1/4" (6mm) presser foot, sometimes called a quilting foot or patchwork foot, is the way to achieve perfect 1/4" (6mm) seams.

All patterns are full-size and located at the back of the book. You can remove the pages for use, photocopy them or trace them.

Thank You for buying my book. This project pairs two of my passions — sewing and dolls. Writing it was a true joy, taking me back to my days of childhood play. If you enjoy my patterns, I would appreciate it so much if you post a brief review at your online place of purchase. Other customers would appreciate it too!

Nothing compares to the thrill of combining a pattern with your own creative fabric selection — and watching that vision come to life. I wish you happy sewing and a delightful new wardrobe for your fashion dolls!

Linda

FASHION DOLL MEASUREMENTS

These patterns are designed for the popular brand of 11½" fashion dolls. Measure your doll's body to compare with the measurements below. If adjustments are needed, allow for them when cutting fabric.

Size & Height.....................................11 1/2" (29cm)
Bust..5" (13cm)
Outer leg length, waist to ankle ....6 3/4" (17cm)
Waist..3 1/2" (9cm)
Hip ....5" (13cm)
Scale..1:6

Patterns are made to fit measurements of 'original' body type Barbie® Made-to-Move™, Fashionista™ and Looks™ dolls.

FABRIC

For the best results when starting out, choose tightly-woven, lightweight, cotton fabrics such as the cotton used for quilts. They will work wonders. On the other hand, fabric that is slippery, very stretchy or unravels easily becomes fiddly to handle when working with tiny seams.

Fancy fabrics, such as satin and taffeta, will elevate the look and add a touch of glamour. These materials are trickier to manipulate, but can be worth the effort. Denim is a must for modern doll clothes, but be sure to find some that is thin. Baby clothes are a good source for denim-look fabric that is ideal for dolls. For prints, choose small-scale motifs that will complement the size of an 11 1/2" (29cm) doll.

Old clothing is a fabulous source of fabric. Check thrift stores, estate sales, garage sales or your own giveaway pile. Look for tiny prints or expensive fabrics, such as silk. Scrap fabric from old leggings and t-shirts makes very realistic hosiery and t-shirts for dolls.

- Fabric stores sell pieces as small as 1/8 yard (12cm).
- Fat Quarters are 18"x21" (50cm x 53cm) quarter-yard pieces of fabric intended for quilts, but perfect for doll clothes. Look for these at fabric stores, craft stores and dollar stores (Dollar Tree in the U.S.).
- Thrift Stores offer a bonanza of baby clothes. These are wonderful sources of lightweight fabrics with small patterns. Explore vintage pillowcases, scarves and handkerchiefs at thrift stores, too.
- Shop at discount stores for baby and toddler clothes. Childrens' underwear is a good weight with cute prints. Even mens' boxers come in interesting fabrics. For online shopping, I use Amazon, Joann Fabric and Etsy. Etsy has quite a few doll clothing shops dedicated to selling small-scale printed fabric, buttons, snaps, buckles and trims.
- For garments using netting, tulle is sold in inexpensive rolls that work well.

♥ **Cutting Plaids & Stripes:** Matching plaids and stripes is good craftsmanship. Align the motifs on both layers of fabric before cutting. The resulting garments will have stripes that cross seamlines, and plaids that appear uninterrupted by seams.

TIPS & TOOLS

♥ **All-Purpose Scissors**: For cutting out paper patterns. Small scissors are good for tight curves.

♥ **Dressmaker's Shears**: For cutting fabric.

♥ **Pinking Shears**: Can be used to trim seam allowances, after a seam is sewn, to prevent raveling, and to help them lay flatter.

♥ **Straight Pins**: For holding patterns to fabric and keeping materials together while you stitch. Thin pins are best for lightweight fabrics.

♥ **Sewing Machine Needles**: Small sizes (10 & 12) are best for the lightweight fabrics used for doll clothes. Ballpoint needles & stretch needles are key to success for sewing knits.

♥ **Loop Turner**: For turning narrow fabric cylinders and tubes right side out. Search 'how to use a loop turner' on YouTube to see demo videos.

♥ **6" (15.2cm) Serrated-Tip Hobby Tweezers**: My go-to for turning pant legs, long sleeves and stockings right side out. Insert tweezers in tunnel, pinch tips on seam allowance and pull through.

♥ **Seam Gauge**: A measuring tool with a sliding marker that stays in place. Very helpful when pressing under narrow hems and casings.

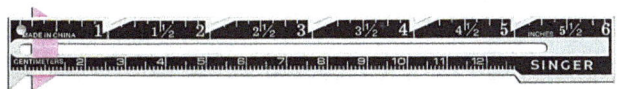

♥ **1/4" (6mm) Presser Foot**: A sewing machine accessory for making accurate 1/4" (6mm) seams. My *clear plastic* 1/4" (6mm) presser foot was a true game changer, providing clear visibility of the fabric under the foot. This makes it much easier to precisely place stitches on the tight curves of tiny garments. Note — Most standard presser feet are wider than 1/4". Don't line up fabric with the edge of this presser foot or the garments will come out too small.

♥ **Disappearing Ink Marking Pen**: For making non-permanent marks on fabric such as darts, dots and other pattern symbols.

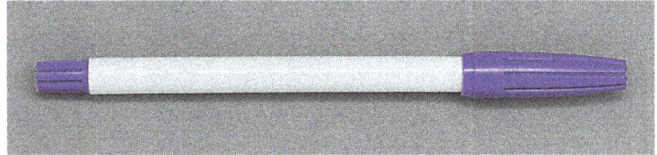

♥ **Tailor's Chalk**: For marking dark fabrics. My sewing box includes 3 types: triangular tailor's chalk, a chalk pencil and a chalk wheel.

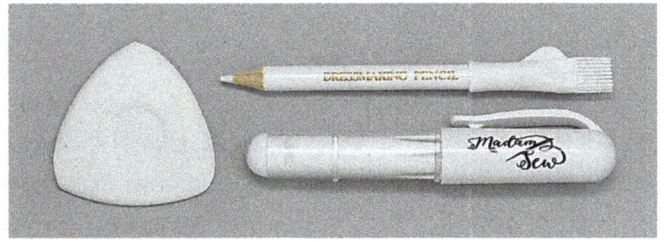

♥ **Glue**: Fabri Tac® is an excellent fabric glue that can be a great aid for attaching straps & adornments. I use an Avery Glue Stic™ for securing turned necklines or sleeveless armholes prior to topstitching. Always test on your fabric first!

♥ **Velcro®**: Sew-on hook-&-loop fastener tape used for closures. Easy for children to manipulate. My favorite for doll clothes is Velcro® Sleek & Thin™. This type is no-snag and won't get tangled in doll hair.

♥ **Snaps**: Closures made from metal or plastic. Can be substituted for Velcro®, if desired.

♥ **Elastic**: Elastic is manufactured as braided or knit. For doll clothes, get *braided*. This provides a firmer hold that stays strong over time.

♥ **Tissue Paper or Wax Paper**: Use under delicate fabric when machine sewing to prevent it from being pulled down into the needle plate. Easy to tear off after. For best results, use a small stitch length.

♥ **Cutting Board**: A folding cardboard cutting board laid on a bed makes a great cutting table and stores compactly! Dritz and Singer make them.

♥ **Thread Dish**: I use a ceramic bowl near my sewing machine to collect the thread tails trimmed off seams while sewing.

GENERAL DIRECTIONS

♥ **SEAM ALLOWANCE** - Patterns include seam allowances. Seam allowances are 1/4" (6mm) unless instructions indicate otherwise. Applicable patterns will indicate a 1/2" (1.2cm) seam allowance at center back to allow extra fabric for fitting the garment to your doll. You can sew that seam with a smaller seam allowance if needed for a good fit. Sometimes small adjustments are needed just because of the properties of the fabric being used.

♥ **STITCH** - With RIGHT sides together, sew 1/4" (6mm) seams and press seams open unless otherwise indicated.

♥ **RIGHT SIDE and WRONG SIDE** - The "right side" of the fabric is meant to be visible from the outside of your garment for everyone to see, while the "wrong side" is the side that will be hidden on the inside of the garment.

♥ **CLIP CURVES or NOTCH CURVES** - When a seam is curved, turning the fabric right side out can cause pulling or wrinkling. To make curved seams lay flat, use the tips of your shears to **clip** or **notch** the seam allowance, taking care not to cut into the stitching.

• **Inner Curve** - Cut small slits or **CLIPS**.

• **Outer Curve** - Cut small V-shaped **NOTCHES**.

♥ **DARTS** - With RIGHT sides of fabric together, bring dotted lines of darts together. Sew along dotted lines from wide end to point.

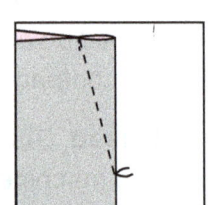

♥ **GATHER** - Sew along the 1/4" (6mm) seamline and 1/8" (3mm) away in the seam allowance, using a long machine stitch.

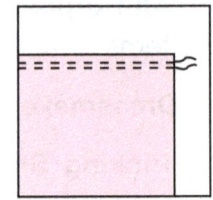

♥ **TRIM OUTER CORNER** - Cut off excess seam allowance at point of corner and at each side.

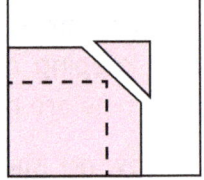

♥ **CLIP INNER CORNER** - Cut a slit into the corner.

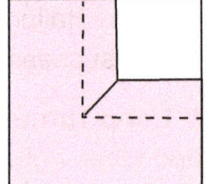

♥ **BACKSTITCHING** - Backstitch at beginning and end of all seams to secure stitching. To backstitch, put machine in reverse and stitch again over previous stitching for about 1/2" (1.3cm).

♥ **STAYSTITCHING** - A reinforcement stitch. Stitch on the stitchline, thru one layer of fabric, with a slightly smaller stitch than normal.

♥ **TOPSTITCHING** - Decorative stitching on the outside of a garment, usually with a straight stitch.

♥ **FINISHING RAW EDGES**

To prevent raveling and make the inside of a garment look nice, raw edges may be finished with pinking shears, a zigzag stitch, serger or Fray Check fabric sealant.

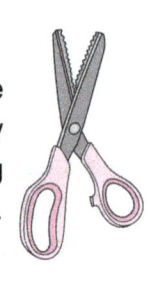

♥ **SPAGHETTI STRAP TIP**

Several patterns include narrow straps. If you find them difficult to handle, try making 1 extra-long strap, then cut to size into 2 straps.

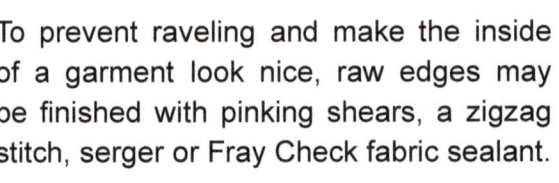

GENERAL DIRECTIONS

♥ FINISHING BACK OPENING EDGES

Use 3/4" wide (19mm) Velcro. If your Velcro includes smooth "sewing lanes" along the sides, cut them off before Step 3.

1. Press under 1/2" (1.2cm) on one side of back opening.

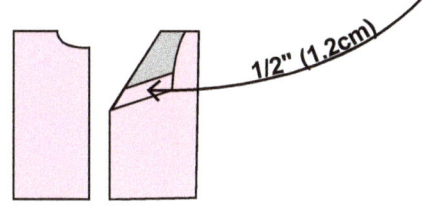

2. Cut a length of Velcro to fit opening.

3. Cut width of Velcro to make strip 3/8" (8mm) wide.

4. Separate halves of Velcro.

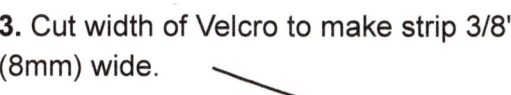

5. Sew **rough side** of Velcro on INSIDE along pressed edge.

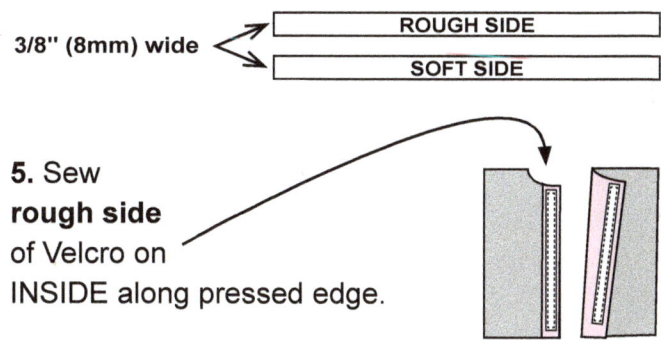

6. Sew **soft side** of Velcro on OUTSIDE of opposite back opening, having one long edge along **center back**, or as needed for best fit.

7. Press seam allowance to one side.

♥ INSERTING ELASTIC

Attach safety pin at end of elastic piece, then push pin into casing. You can feel the end of the safety pin and slide it forward, gathering up the fabric, then pulling the excess fabric back behind the pin. Work the safety pin through in this manner, inching it through the casing until it appears on the other end of the tunnel.

♥ PRESSING

Pressing as you sew is crucial for a professional outcome. Pressing sets stitches into the fabric, flattens seams for less bulk, makes seams less visible, and shapes the garment. To press your sewn pieces, lift the iron and  place it gently down on a specific area, then lift it and move it again. It's an up-and-down motion rather than a side-to-side motion. I use a standard iron and ironing board for doll clothes, but small versions of both are available, if preferred.

Tip: To make a **Seam Roll** for pressing small cylinders such as pant legs and sleeves, roll a thin catalog or a piece of cardstock tightly. It will expand to fit the space perfectly.

♥ ALTERATIONS

If your fashion doll has slightly different proportions from the measurements on page 6, follow these tips.

• **Enlarge:** Add extra fabric at the side seams when you cut.

• **Reduce:** Sew with a slightly larger seam allowance to take in the fit.

• **Lengthen:** Before cutting the fabric, extend the pattern at the hem or sleeve edge by the desired amount.

• **Shorten:** Trim the hem or sleeve edge before sewing.

FLOWER POWER DRESS

The strapless dress with a gathered waist is adorned with a ribbon flower.

SUPPLIES

Satin, taffeta or lightweight woven cotton fabric, 1/8 yd (.11m)

7/8" (2.2cm) wide satin ribbon

1 crystal self-adhesive acrylic gem, 10mm

3/4" (19mm) wide Velcro®Sleek&Thin™ sew-on tape

Hot glue, optional

Note: PATTERN IS ON PAGE 61. Pattern includes seam allowances. Seam allowances are 1/4" (6mm) unless instructions indicate otherwise.

DRESS

1. Press BODICE on foldline with WRONG sides together. Sew darts thru both layers. Press darts toward center.

2. To gather SKIRT, machine baste 1/4" and 1/8" (6mm and 3mm) from upper edge.

3. Press under 1/4" (6mm) hem on lower edge of skirt. Sew 1/8" (3mm) from pressed edge.

4. With RIGHT sides together, pin skirt to bodice at waistline seam, matching centers and having back edges even. Pull up bobbin threads and adjust gathers to fit. Sew in place. Press seam allowance toward bodice.

5. Sew up center back of skirt, **1/2" (1.2cm)** from edge, stitching from hem to DOT (see pattern).

6. Apply fasteners; see FINISHING BACK OPENING EDGES, page 9. ♥

FLOWER

The flower is made with hand-sewing.

1. Cut a 12" piece of ribbon. Gather ribbon with running stitch close to one long edge, making a backstitch at the first stitch to secure the thread.

2. Pull gathers tight, bringing ends together to form a circle. Secure with a knot. Sew raw edges together with a narrow seam.

3. Attach gem to center of flower.

4. Sew or glue flower to center front of bodice. ♥

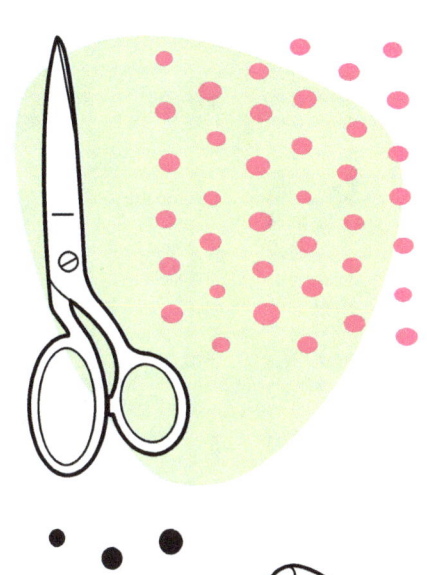

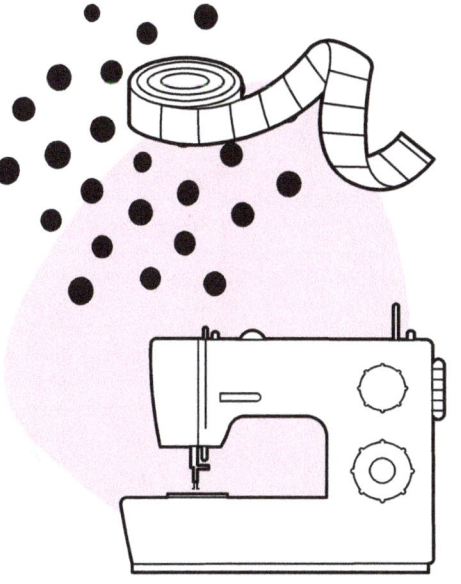

11

SHIFT DRESS

This very easy pattern is a great starter project. See the dress pictured with a Denim Jacket on Page 43.

SUPPLIES

Lightweight woven or knit cotton fabric, 1/4 yd (.23m)

3/4" (19mm) wide Velcro® Sleek & Thin™ sew-on tape

All purpose glue stick, optional

Note: PATTERN IS ON PAGE 63. Pattern includes seam allowances. Seam allowances are 1/4" (6mm) unless instructions indicate otherwise.

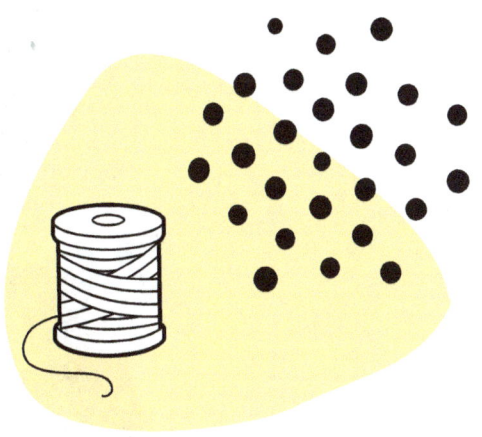

1. With RIGHT sides together, stitch FRONT to BACK at shoulders.

2. Press under 1/4" (6mm) on edge of armholes. Sew 1/8" (3mm) from pressed edge.

3. To hem neckline, machine stitch 1/4" (6mm) from edge. Press or glue* under on stitchline, clipping curves. Sew in place 1/8" (3mm) from turned edge.
* Note: To glue, lightly dab glue stick along wrong side of seam allowance and finger-press in place.

4. With RIGHT sides together, stitch side seams.

5. Press under 1/4" (6mm) hem on lower edge of dress. Sew 1/8" (3mm) from pressed edge.

6. With RIGHT sides together, sew up center back of dress, **1/2" (1.2cm)** from edge, stitching from hem to DOT (see pattern).

7. Apply fasteners; see FINISHING BACK OPENING EDGES, page 9. ♥

STRAIGHT SKIRT, BANDEAU & FINGERLESS GLOVES

A bold-colored skirt with matching bandeau and fingerless gloves makes a stunning outfit. Knit fabric is used to get the stretch needed for the gloves, but try to find a firm knit. If your fabric is too stretchy, the bandeau can be fiddly to make. In that case, interface the bandeau fabric, before cutting, with fusible interfacing such as Heat-n-Bond Lite Weight Non-Woven. The center strap of the bandeau fastens at the back of the neck.

SUPPLIES

Lightweight knit fabric, 1/4 yd (.23m)

1/4" (6mm) wide braided elastic

3/4" (19mm) wide Velcro® Sleek & Thin™ sew-on tape

Fabric glue

Note: PATTERNS ARE ON PAGE 65. Pattern includes seam allowances. Seam allowances are 1/4" (6mm) unless instructions indicate otherwise.

STRAIGHT SKIRT

1. Press under 1/4" (6mm) hem on lower edge of SKIRT. Sew 1/8" (3mm) from pressed edge.

2. For casing, press under 1/2" (1.2cm) at upper edge of skirt. Sew 3/8" (1cm) from pressed edge.

3. Cut elastic 3 1/2" (9cm) long. Using a small safety pin, insert elastic thru casing and sew securely at ends.

4. With RIGHT sides together, stitch center back seam. ♥

BANDEAU

1. Press under 1/4" (6mm) on both long edges of STRAP. Fold strap in half lengthwise, WRONG sides together and press again. Sew lengthwise along center thru all layers.

2. Press under 1/4" (6mm) on upper and lower edges of BANDEAU. Sew 1/8" (3mm) from pressed edges.

3. Hand-gather along center front using a double thread in your needle. Pull up gathering stitches tight. Fasten thread securely.

4. Referring to photo on previous page, fold strap in half and insert bandeau at loop end. Sew or glue in place.

5. Cut small Velcro patches to fit ends of neck strap. Glue in place.

6. Apply fastener to back of bandeau; see FINISHING BACK OPENING EDGES, page 9, Steps 1-6. ♥

FINGERLESS GLOVES

1. Press under 1/4" (6mm) on upper and lower edge of each GLOVE. Sew 1/8" (3mm) from pressed edges.

2. With RIGHT sides together, fold gloves lengthwise so that raw edges meet and stitch seam. ♥

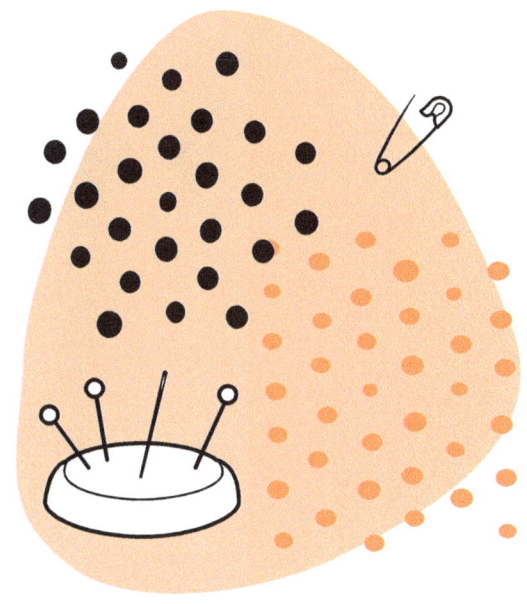

SPAGHETTI STRAP SWING DRESS

The combination of a full-circle skirt and box pleats makes this dress especially full and swingy. My cutting was planned so the bodice would have a large flower at center front. The belt buckle is easy to make from craft wire or a paper clip.

SUPPLIES

Lightweight woven cotton fabric, 3/8 yd (.34m)
3/4" (19mm) wide Velcro® Sleek & Thin™ sew-on tape
Paper clip or 18 gauge craft wire; pencil, wire cutters and file
1 snap

Note: PATTERN IS ON PAGES 67-69. Pattern includes seam allowances. Seam allowances are 1/4" (6mm) unless instructions indicate otherwise.

1. To staystitch BODICE, sew 1/4" (6mm) from upper edge. Press under 1/4" (6mm) using the stitchline for a guide, clipping to staystitching at center front. Sew 1/8" (3mm) from pressed edge.

2. Sew bodice darts. Press darts toward center.

3. On SKIRT, cut center back open along foldline.

4. To mark pleats, make tiny clips at red lines on pattern, being careful not to clip thru seamline.

5. To make pleats, on OUTSIDE, fold along solid lines. Bring folds to dotted lines and pin. (Follow **Fig. A** or arrows on pattern for direction of pleats.) Baste pleats in place.

6. To make guideline for hem, sew around lower edge of skirt 1/4" (6mm) from edge. Press fabric under on guideline. Sew 1/8" (3mm) from pressed edge.

7. With RIGHT sides together, pin skirt to bodice at waistline seam, matching centers and back edges. Stitch in place. Press seam allowance toward bodice.

8. On STRAPS, press under 1/8" (3mm) on long edges. Fold in half lengthwise, WRONG sides together, and press again. Sew lengthwise along middle of straps thru all layers.

9. Lap upper edge of bodice 1/4" (6mm) over straps at DOTS (see pattern), being careful not to twist straps. Sew straps in place.

10. With RIGHT sides together, sew up center back of skirt, **1/2" (1.2cm) from edge**, stitching from hem to DOT (see pattern).

11. Apply fasteners to **bodice**; see FINISHING BACK OPENING EDGES, page 9.

12. Press under 1/4" (6mm) on all 4 edges of BELT. Fold in half lengthwise, WRONG sides together and press again. Sew lengthwise along center thru all layers.

13. For BUCKLE, wrap wire once around a pencil to make a ring (X). Slide ring off pencil and bend tail of wire across center to make a bar (Y). Trim away excess with wire cutters (Z). Smooth cuts with a file. Thread belt thru buckle, positioning buckle at center. Sew snap to ends of belt. ♥

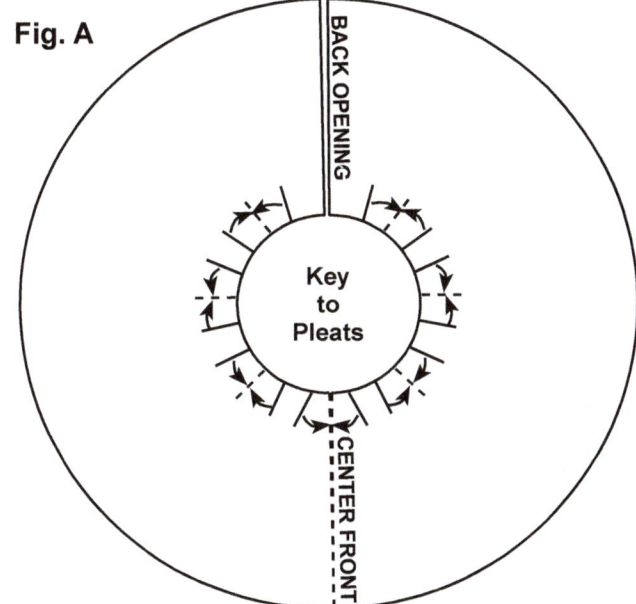

Fig. A

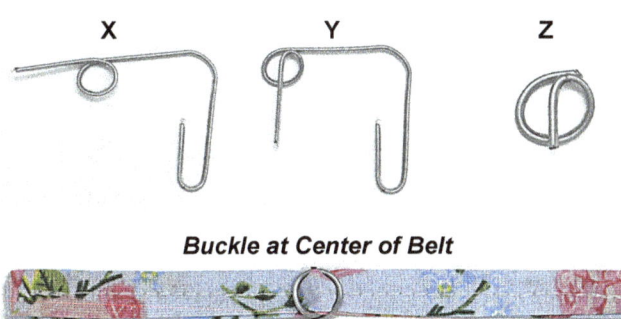

Buckle at Center of Belt

OVERSHIRT, T-SHIRT & MOCK-DRAWSTRING SHORTS

SUPPLIES

Lightweight woven cotton fabric, 1/4 yd (.23m) for Shorts & Overshirt
Lightweight cotton knit fabric, 1/8 yd (.11m) for T-Shirt
3/4" (19mm) wide Velcro® Sleek & Thin™ sew-on tape
1/8" wide braided elastic
String or yarn
4 buttons, 1/4" (6mm)
4 snaps, optional

Note: PATTERNS ARE ON PAGES 71-73. Pattern includes seam allowances. Seam allowances are 1/4" (6mm) unless instructions indicate otherwise.

OVERSHIRT

1. To make FACING, press under 1/2" (1.2cm) on front edge of SHIRT FRONTS (see foldline on pattern). Tuck raw edge under to meet crease. Press. Sew facing in place.

2. Sew front sections to BACK at shoulder seams. Press seams toward back. On OUTSIDE, topstitch back close to shoulder seams.

3. Press under 1/4" (6mm) on lower edge of sleeves. Sew 1/8" (3mm) from pressed edges.

4. Press under 1/4" (6mm) on one long edge of COLLAR. With RIGHT sides together, fold collar lengthwise on foldline (see pattern). Sew across ends. Trim corners.

5. Turn collar RIGHT side out. Press.

6. To staystitch, machine stitch around neck edge of shirt, using a short stitch length. Clip to stitching. With RIGHT sides together, pin raw edge of collar to neck edge of shirt. Sew in place taking care to keep pressed edge of collar free. Clip curves.

7. On INSIDE, hand sew pressed edge of collar over neck seam with slip stitch.

8. Stitch fronts to back at entire underarm seams. Clip curves.

9. Press under 1/2" (1.2cm) hem on lower edge of shirt. Tuck raw edge under to meet crease. Press. Sew hem in place.

10. Sew buttons to one front edge. Optional: Sew snaps to shirt under buttons with corresponding section of snaps on opposite edge of shirt. ♥

T-SHIRT

1. With RIGHT sides together, stitch FRONT to BACK at shoulders.

2. With WRONG sides together, press neckband in half lengthwise.

3. With RIGHT sides together, pin long raw edge of neckband to neckline of SHIRT. Stitch in place. Press seam toward shirt. On OUTSIDE, topstitch shirt near seam.

4. Press under 1/4" (6mm) on lower edge of SLEEVES. Sew 1/8" (3mm) from pressed edge.

5. With RIGHT sides together, pin each sleeve to armhole edge of shirt. Stitch in place. Press seam toward sleeve.

6. With RIGHT sides together, stitch front to backs at entire underarm seam, matching armhole seams.

7. Press under 1/4" (6mm) hem on lower edge of shirt. Sew 1/8" (3mm) from pressed edge.

8. Apply fasteners; see FINISHING BACK OPENING EDGES, page 9, Steps 1-6. ♥

MOCK-DRAWSTRING SHORTS

1. With RIGHT sides together, stitch center front seam. Clip curves.

2. Press under 1/4" (6mm) hem on lower edge of shorts. Sew 1/8" (3mm) from pressed edge.

3. For casing, press under 1/2" (1.2cm) on upper edge. Sew 3/8" (8mm) from pressed edge.

4. Cut elastic 3 1/2" (9cm) long. Using a small safety pin, insert elastic thru casing and sew securely at ends.

5. With RIGHT sides together, stitch center back seam. Clip curves.

6. With RIGHT sides together, stitch front to back at inseam, matching center seams.

7. For MOCK-DRAWSTRING, cut a short length of string. Sew center of string to center front of waistline casing. Tie in a bow and trim tails. ♥

PRINCESS DRESS

Every little girl's fashion doll needs a Princess Dress! In this pattern, a hidden skirt provides the foundation for 4 rows of ruffles. The dress can be made strapless, if desired.

SUPPLIES

Lightweight woven cotton fabric, taffeta or satin, 1/4 yd (.23m) for bodice, skirt and Ruffle 1

Lightweight woven cotton fabric, taffeta or satin, 1/8 yd (.11m) for Ruffles 2, 3 and 4

Sequin trim 1/4" (6mm) wide

3/4" (19mm) wide Velcro® Sleek & Thin™ sew-on tape

Fabric glue

Note: PATTERN IS ON PAGES 75-79. Pattern includes seam allowances. Seam allowances are 1/4" (6mm) unless instructions indicate otherwise.

1. Press BODICE on foldline with WRONG sides together. Sew darts thru both layers. Press darts toward center.

2. With RIGHT sides together, stitch SKIRT BACK sections to SKIRT FRONT at sides.

3. Press under 1/4" (6mm) hem on lower edge of skirt. Sew 1/8" (3mm) from pressed edge.

4. Press under 1/4" (6mm) hem on one long edge of all RUFFLES. Sew 1/8" (3mm) from pressed edge.

5. To gather upper edge of ruffles, machine-baste 1/4" and 1/8" (6mm and 3mm) from other long edge.

6. With RIGHT SIDES UP, pin Ruffle 4 to skirt along lowest placement line, matching center fronts and back edges, and having lowest row of gathering stitches along the placement line. Pull up bobbin threads and adjust gathers to fit. Sew 1/4" (6mm) from raw edge.

Pin and sew Ruffles 3 and 2 to remaining placement lines in same manner.

Pin and sew Ruffle 1 to waistline of skirt in same manner with raw edges even.

7. Pin skirt to bodice, RIGHT sides together, matching center fronts and back edges. Stitch in place. Press seam allowance toward bodice.

8. With RIGHT sides together, pin center back seam of skirt making sure raw edges of skirt and ruffles align so ruffles are caught in seam. Sew **1/2" (1.2cm)** from edge, stitching from hem to DOT (see pattern).

9. Apply fasteners to **bodice**; see FINISHING BACK OPENING EDGES, page 9, Steps 1-6.

10. On STRAPS, press under 1/8" (3mm) on long edges. Fold in half lengthwise, WRONG sides together, and press again. Sew lengthwise along middle of straps thru all layers.

11. Lap upper edge of bodice 1/4" (6mm) over straps at DOTS (see pattern), being careful not to twist straps. Sew straps in place.

12. Cut sequin trim to fit straps and upper edge of bodice. Glue in place. ♥

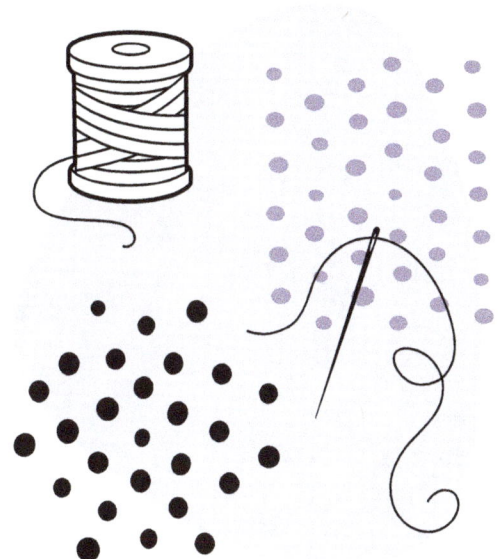

WRAP COAT

The key to this easy coat is polyester fleece, also known as polar fleece. Fleece won't fray or ravel, so the edges can be left unhemmed.

SUPPLIES
Medium-weight polyester fleece, 1/3 yd (.30m)

Note: PATTERN IS ON PAGE 81. Pattern includes seam allowances. Seam allowances are 1/4" (6mm) unless instructions indicate otherwise.

1. With RIGHT sides together, stitch center back seam. Trim seam allowance to 1/8" (3mm).

2. With RIGHT sides together, stitch entire underarm seams of coat and sleeves, pivoting needle at underarm corner. Clip seam allowance at corners. Trim seam allowance to 1/8" (3mm).

3. With WRONG sides together, pin COLLAR against inside of coat, with neck edges aligned, matching center backs, between DOTS (see pattern). Sew in place 1/8" from edge with machine zigzag or by hand with whipstitch.

4. Fold lapels on creaselines. ♥

TRAPEZOID PURSE

The purse is quick and easy to make. A bead is used for a button closure. Find your felt scraps and make purses to match every outfit!

SUPPLIES
Felt
1 bead
Fabric glue

Note: PATTERN IS ON PAGE 81. Pattern includes seam allowances. Seam allowances are 1/4" (6mm).

1. For HANDLES, cut 2 strips of felt 1/8" (3mm) x 2 3/4" (7cm).

2. With RIGHT sides together, crease purse on foldline and sew side seams.

3. On INSIDE, to form rectangular bottom, finger-press side seams open and fold bottom ends as shown in Fig. A. Stitch 1/4" (6mm) from tips, thru all layers, as shown by dotted line below. Turn purse right-side out.

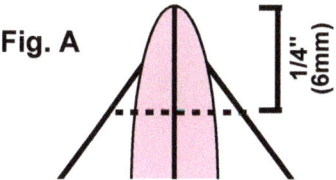

Fig. A

4. For closure, cut a small slit in flap (see pattern). Sew bead to purse under slit.

5. Lap ends of handles 1/4" (6mm) over upper edge of purse at DOTS (see pattern), being careful not to twist handles. Glue in place. ♥

PEPLUM BLOUSE & LEGGINGS

The fabric used for the pictured outfit is cotton knit upcycled from a baby dress. The cutting was planned so a large spray of flowers would be positioned at the center-front of the bodice.

Some zigzag stitching is used in this outfit to retain the stretch of the knit and prevent the hem edges from rolling.

Due to their tiny size, the necklines of fashion doll clothes can be tricky to machine staystitch, turn under, press and sew. You can turn the raw edge under and glue it in place with fabric glue, if preferred. Be sure to test your glue first on a scrap to be sure it doesn't soak thru and leave marks.

SUPPLIES

Lightweight knit fabric, 1/4 yd (.23m)

1/4" (6mm) wide braided elastic

3/4" (19mm) wide Velcro® Sleek & Thin™ sew-on tape

All purpose glue stick, optional

Note: PATTERNS ARE ON PAGE 83. Pattern includes seam allowances. Seam allowances are 1/4" (6mm) unless instructions indicate otherwise.

PEPLUM BLOUSE

1. With RIGHT sides together, stitch front to back at shoulders.

2. On neckline, machine stitch 1/4" (6mm) from edge. Press or glue* under on stitchline, clipping curves. Sew 1/8" (3mm) from turned edge.
* Note: To glue, lightly dab glue stick along wrong side of seam allowance and finger-press in place.

3. Press under 1/4" (6mm) on ends of sleeves. Sew over raw edge using a zigag stitch at a *long wide* setting.

4. With RIGHT sides together, stitch entire seam of underarms and sides. Clip seam allowance at armpit.

5. Press under 1/4" (6mm) on lower edge of PEPLUM. Sew over raw edge using a zigag stitch at a *long wide* setting.

6. To gather upper edge of peplum, machine baste 1/4" and 1/8" (6mm and 3mm) from raw edge.

7. Pin peplum to bodice, RIGHT sides together, matching centers and having back edges even. Pull up bobbin threads and adjust gathers to fit. Stitch in place. Press seam allowance toward bodice.

8. Apply fasteners; see FINISHING BACK OPENING EDGES, page 9, Steps 1-6. ♥

LEGGINGS

1. With RIGHT sides together, stitch center front seam with a *long narrow* zigzag stitch. Trim seam allowance to 1/8" (3mm).

2. For casing, press under 1/2" (1.2cm) along upper edge. Sew over raw edge using a zigag stitch at a *long wide* setting.

3. Cut elastic 4" (10cm) long. Using a safety pin, insert elastic thru casing and sew securely at ends.

4. Press under 1/4" (6mm) hem at lower edges of leggings. Sew over raw edge using a zigag stitch at a *long wide* setting.

5. With RIGHT sides together, stitch center back seam using a zigzag stitch at a *long narrow* setting. Trim seam allowance to 1/8" (3mm).

6. With RIGHT sides together, stitch inner leg seam using a zigzag stitch at a *long narrow* setting. Trim seam allowance to 1/8" (3mm). ♥

CHRISTMAS TREE SET

A ruffled skirt and a bra top embellished with a bow comprise the festive Christmas outfit.

SUPPLIES

Taffeta or lightweight woven cotton, 3/8 yd (.34m)
Tulle, 1/2 yd (.46m)
7/8" (2.2cm) wide double-faced satin ribbon
3/4" (19mm) wide Velcro®Sleek& Thin™ sew-on tape
1 snap
1/4" (6mm) craft pom-poms
Fabric glue or 3/16" (5mm) permanent glue dots

Note: PATTERN IS ON PAGES 85-89. Pattern includes seam allowances. Seam allowances are 1/4" (6mm) unless instructions indicate otherwise.

SKIRT

1. With RIGHT sides together, stitch SKIRT BACK sections to SKIRT FRONT at sides.

2. Press under 1/4" (6mm) hem on lower edge of skirt. Sew 1/8" (3mm) from pressed edge.

3. Press under 1/4" (6mm) hem on one long edge of FABRIC RUFFLES (not tulle ruffles). Sew 1/8" (3mm) from pressed edge.

4. Stack two TULLE RUFFLES on RIGHT side of each corresponding fabric ruffle with raw edges even. Pin in place. To gather upper edge of ruffles, machine-baste 1/4" and 1/8" (6mm and 3mm) from raw edge thru all layers.

5. With RIGHT SIDES UP, pin Ruffle 4 to skirt along lowest placement line, matching center fronts and back edges, and having lowest row of gathering stitches along the placement line. Pull up bobbin threads and adjust gathers to fit. Sew 1/4" (6mm) from raw edge.

Pin and sew Ruffles 3 and 2 to remaining placement lines in same manner.

Pin and sew Ruffle 1 to waistline of skirt in same manner with raw edges even. Trim seam allowance.

6. Pin WAISTBAND to skirt, RIGHT sides together, matching center fronts & back edges. Sew in place. Press under 1/4" on other long edge of waistband. Fold pressed edge over seam allowance to meet stitchline. Sew in place by hand with whip stitch.

7. With RIGHT sides together, pin center back seam making sure raw edges of skirt and ruffles align so ruffles are caught in seam. Sew **1/2" (1.2cm)** from edge, stitching from hem to DOT (see pattern).

8. Turn under 1/2" (1.2cm) on one back opening edge. Sew prong half of SNAP to INSIDE on waistband. Sew socket half of snap to OUTSIDE on opposite end of waistband.

9. Attach POM POMS to skirt with fabric glue or glue dots. ♥

BRA

1. Press under 1/4" (6mm) on upper & lower edges of BRA. Sew 1/8" (3mm) from pressed edges.

2. Hand-gather along center front using a double thread in your needle. Wrap thread around gathers twice and knot securely.

3. Press under 1/4" (6mm) on both long edges of STRAPS. Fold straps in half lengthwise, WRONG sides together and press again. Sew lengthwise along center of each strap thru all layers.

4. Lap upper edge of bra 1/4" (6mm) over straps at DOTS (see pattern), being careful not to twist straps. Sew in place.

5. Apply fastener; see FINISHING BACK OPENING EDGES, page 9, Steps 1-6. ♥

BOW

The bow is made with hand-sewing.

1. Wrap SECTION 1 into a loop so ribbon ends overlap each other by 1" (2.5cm). Flatten loop at center of overlap. Using a double thread in your needle, gather across center of overlap thru all layers. Pull gathers tight, wrap thread around gathers twice & knot securely. Do NOT cut thread.

2. Fold SECTION 2 in thirds by folding selvage edges inward (see dotted lines on pattern). Wrap this around middle of Section 1, butting cut ends together at back of bow, and joining with whip stitch. Do NOT cut thread.

3. Crease SECTION 3 on foldline (see pattern) and press. Sew to back of bow.

4. Sew or glue bow to center front of bra. ♥

STRAIGHT-LEG JEANS

Use gold thread for the decorative topstitching.

SUPPLIES
Lightweight denim fabric, 1/4 yd (.23m)
1 snap
1 gold button, 1/4" (6mm)
Chalk fabric pencil, optional

Note: PATTERN IS ON PAGE 91. Pattern includes seam allowances. Seam allowances are 1/4" (6mm) unless instructions indicate otherwise.

1. Sew darts on back sections. Press darts toward center.

2. For mock fly, topstitch one jeans front as shown on patttern with dashed lines. For mock pockets, topstitch jeans fronts & backs as shown with dashed lines. *Templates are provided that you can position to draw stitchlines with a white chalk pencil.*

3. With RIGHT sides together, sew fronts to backs at sides. Press seam toward back.

4. On OUTSIDE, topstitch backs along side seams, stitching close to the seam.

5. With RIGHT sides together, stitch center front seam of jeans front sections. Clip curves.

6. To staystitch waistline, sew 1/4" (6mm) from edge. Clip to stitching. Press under on stitchline and topstitch close to pressed edge.

7. Press under 1/4" (6mm) hem on bottom of pant legs. Topstitch 1/8" from pressed edges.

8. With RIGHT sides together, sew center back seam of jeans back sections BETWEEN DOTS with **1/2" (1.2cm)** seam allowance, leaving an opening above dots. Trim seam allowance to 1/4" between dots. Clip curves.

9. With RIGHT sides together, stitch fronts to backs at inner leg edges matching crotch seams.

10. Press under 1/2" (1.2cm) on one back opening edge. Sew prong half of snap fastener to one upper corner and socket half to corresponding corner.

11. Sew button to upper edge at fly. ♥

FLARED TOP

SUPPLIES
Lightweight woven cotton fabric, 1/8 yd (.11m)
3/4" (19mm) wide Velcro® Sleek & Thin™ sew-on tape
All purpose glue stick, optional

Note: PATTERN IS ON PAGE 91. Pattern includes seam allowances. Seam allowances are 1/4" (6mm) unless instructions indicate otherwise.

1. With RIGHT sides together, sew front to back at shoulders.

2. To hem neckline, machine stitch 1/4" (6mm) from edge. Press or glue* under on stitchline, clipping curves. Sew in place 1/8" (3mm) from turned edge.

* Note: To glue, lightly dab glue stick along wrong side of seam allowance and finger-press in place.

3. Clip front and back to DOTS (see pattern). Press under 1/4" (6mm) between clips. Sew 1/8" from pressed edge.

4. With RIGHT sides together, stitch side seams.

5. Press under 1/4" (6mm) hem on lower edge of shirt. Sew 1/8" (3mm) from pressed edge.

6. Apply fasteners; see FINISHING BACK OPENING EDGES, page 9, Steps 1-6. ♥

SOCK SHEATH DRESS

This form-fitting dress is made from a single sock. I enjoy using socks with playful designs. Holiday socks are perfect for making seasonal dresses.

Fusible tape is used here. I found it to be the best way to get a smooth hem on such stretchy fabric. Various fusible tapes are available. The one I used is SewkeysE "Extremely Fine Double Sided Fusible Stay Tape". Follow the instructions included with your product.

For the best results, use a ballpoint needle and a zigzag stitch. The inherent stretch of zigzag will allow the dress to stretch without popping a seam.

SUPPLIES

1 knee-high sock

Double-sided fusible tape, 1/4" (6mm) wide

Note: PATTERN IS ON PAGE 93. Pattern includes seam allowances. Seam allowances are 1/4" (6mm) unless instructions indicate otherwise.

1. Position pattern so that Top is along upper edge of sock. Cut out.

2. On each DRESS piece, press fusible tape to WRONG side along raw edge of hemline. Do not peel away the protective paper backing yet.

3. With RIGHT sides together, sew side seams.

4. Peel paper backing from fusible tape. Press under 1/4" (6mm) hem. Sew 1/8" (3mm) from pressed edge.

5. Trim side seam allowances to 1/8" (3mm). ♥

RUNWAY DRESS

This dress is created in 2 pieces as a strapless mini dress with an overskirt that snaps in place. Volume is created in both pieces with soft pleats. To mark the pleats, as soon as you cut a pattern piece from fabric (before removing pins), make 1/8" (3mm) clips into the seam allowance for each pleat line. Then match the clips according to the pattern to pin each pleat. The satin used for the dress pictured was very thin, so I reinforced the bodice fabric, before cutting, with fusible interfacing (Heat-n-Bond Lite Weight Non-Woven). This helped support the overskirt. Runway Dresses made from sturdier fabrics were fine without interfacing.

SUPPLIES

Lightweight woven cotton, satin or taffeta, 1/4 yd (.23m)
3/4" (19mm) wide Velcro® Sleek & Thin™ sew-on tape
2 snaps

Note: PATTERN IS ON PAGES 93-95. Pattern includes seam allowances. Seam allowances are 1/4" (6mm) unless instructions indicate otherwise.

DRESS

1. Press BODICE on foldline with WRONG sides together. Sew darts thru both layers. Press darts toward center.

2. Press under 1/4" (6mm) on lower edge of SKIRT. Sew 1/8" (3mm) from pressed edge.

3. To make soft pleats, on OUTSIDE, fold along solid lines; bring folds to broken lines and pin in place following arrows on pattern for direction of pleats. Baste pleats.

4. With RIGHT sides together, pin skirt to bodice at waistline seam, matching centers and back edges. Stitch in place. Press seam allowance toward bodice. On OUTSIDE, topstitch bodice close to waistline seam.

5. Sew up center back of skirt from hem to DOT (see pattern), **1/2" (1.2cm) from edge.**

6. Apply fasteners; see FINISHING BACK OPENING EDGES, page 9. ♥

OVERSKIRT

1. Press under 1/8" (3mm) on lower edge of overskirt. Press under again 1/4" (6mm). Sew in place.

2. Press under 1/8" (3mm) on front edges of overskirt. Press under again 1/4" (6mm). Sew in place.

3. To make soft pleats, on OUTSIDE, fold along solid lines; bring folds to broken lines and pin in place following arrows on pattern for direction of pleats. Baste pleats.

4. With RIGHT sides together, pin overskirt to one long edge of waistband, matching centers and placing ends of skirt 1/2" (1.2cm) from ends of waistband. Sew together.

5. Fold waistband to INSIDE over seam, turning under 1/2" (1.2cm) on ends and 1/4" (6mm) on remaining long edge. Hand sew band along seam and ends with slip stitch.

6. Sew prong half of snaps at ends of waistband on INSIDE and socket half of snaps at corresponding location on OUTSIDE of dress front. ♥

SKIRTED BIKINI & BEACH TOWEL

The bikini features a skirted bottom. On the bra top, a strap attaches around the doll's neck.

Tea towels make great beach towels for fashion dolls. Look for stripes or a tropical print.

SUPPLIES

Lightweight woven cotton fabric, 1/4 yd (.23m), for Bikini

Tea towel, for Beach Towel

3/4" (19mm) wide Velcro®Sleek&Thin™ sew-on tape

1/8" (6 mm) wide braided elastic

Fabric glue

Note: PATTERN IS ON PAGE 97. Pattern includes seam allowances. Seam allowances are 1/4" (6mm) unless instructions indicate otherwise.

SKIRTED PANTY

1. On SKIRT, cut center back along slash line and cut out inner circle. To staystitch, sew 1/4" (6mm) from edge around hemline. Notch curves. Press under 1/4" on stitchline. To hem, sew 1/8" (3mm) from pressed edge.

2. Press under 1/4" (6mm) on center-back edges of skirt. Sew 1/8" (3mm) from pressed edges.

3. To staystitch, sew 1/4" (6mm) from edge around waistline of skirt. Clip curves.

4. On PANTY, to staystitch, sew 1/4" (6mm) from edge along leg openings. Clip curves. Press under on stitchline. Sew 1/8" (3mm) from pressed edges.

5. Pin WRONG side of skirt to RIGHT side of panty at waistline, between DOTS (see panty pattern), with center fronts aligned. Baste in place.

6. With WRONG sides together, fold WAISTBAND in half lengthwise. Press.

7. Pin raw edge of waistband to raw edge of skirt. Sew in place thru all layers. Press seam down.

8. Cut elastic 3 1/2" (9cm) long. Using a small safety pin, insert elastic thru waistband casing and sew securely at ends.

9. With RIGHT sides together, stitch center back seam along panty and waistband, using care to keep skirt free.

10. Stitch crotch seam. Place skirted panty on doll, spray lightly with water and squeeze skirt against doll to shape the fullness of the flare. Let dry on doll. ♥

BRA TOP

1. On STRAP, press under 1/4" (6mm) on short ends AND on long edges. Fold strap in half lengthwise, WRONG sides together and press again. Sew lengthwise along center thru all layers.

2. Press under 1/4" (6mm) on upper and lower edges of bra. Sew 1/8" (3mm) from pressed edges.

3. Hand-gather along center front using a double thread in your needle. Pull up gathering stitches tight. Fasten thread securely.

4. Fold strap into a V-shape. On INSIDE, sew or glue tip of V at center front of bra.

5. Cut Velcro into small patches to fit ends of neck strap and glue in place.

6. Apply fastener to back of bra; see FINISHING BACK OPENING EDGES, page 9, Steps 1-6. ♥

BEACH TOWEL

1. Cut an 8"x14" (20x36cm) rectangle from tea towel.

2. Press under 1" (2.5cm) on long sides. Tuck raw edge under to meet crease. Press. Sew in place.

3. Press under 1" (2.5cm) on short sides. Tuck raw edge under to meet crease. Press. Sew in place. ♥

PALAZZO PANTS & RUFFLED BLOUSE

The Palazzo Pants are intended to be low-rise to allow some midriff to show. Check the fit of your elastic before securing it.

SUPPLIES

Lightweight woven cotton fabric, 3/8 yd (.34m)
3/4" (19mm) wide Velcro® Sleek & Thin™ sew-on tape
1/8" (6mm) wide braided elastic
All purpose glue stick, optional

Note: PATTERN IS ON PAGE 99. Pattern includes seam allowances. Seam allowances are 1/4" (6mm) unless instructions indicate otherwise.

PALAZZO PANTS

1. With RIGHT sides together, stitch center front seam. Clip curve.

2. For casing, press under 1/2" (1.3cm) on upper edge. Sew 3/8" (9mm) from pressed edge.

3. Cut elastic 4 1/2" (11cm) long. Using a small safety pin, insert elastic thru casing and sew securely at ends.

4. Press under 1/4" (6mm) on lower edges of pants. Sew 1/8" from pressed edges.

5. With RIGHT sides together, stitch center back seam. Clip curve.

6. With RIGHT sides together, stitch front to back at inside leg edges. ♥

RUFFLED BLOUSE

1. On neckline, machine stitch 1/4" (6mm) from edge. Press or glue* under on stitchline, clipping curves. Sew 1/8" (3mm) from turned edge.
* Note: To glue, lightly dab glue stick along wrong side of seam allowance and finger-press in place.

2. On SIDES, press under 1/4" (6mm) along armholes. Sew 1/8" (3mm) from pressed edge.

3. Press under 1/4" (6mm) on outer curve of RUFFLES. Sew 1/8" (3mm) from pressed edge.

4. To gather inner curve of ruffles, machine baste 1/4" and 1/8" (6mm and 3mm) from raw edge between dots (see pattern).

5. With RIGHT sides together, pin gathered edge of ruffle to outer edge of BODICE. Pull up gathers and adjust to fit. Sew in place.

6. With RIGHT sides together, pin raw edge of sides to raw edge of bodice, over ruffle. Sew in place thru all layers. Trim seam allowance to 1/8" (3mm).

7. With RIGHT sides together, sew side seams. Be careful not to catch ruffle in seam.

8. Press seam allowance of ruffle toward bodice. Press under 1/4" (6mm) hem on lower edge of blouse, lapping front ruffle over back ruffle. Sew 1/8" (3mm) from pressed edge.

9. Apply fasteners; see FINISHING BACK OPENING EDGES, page 9, Steps 1-6. ♥

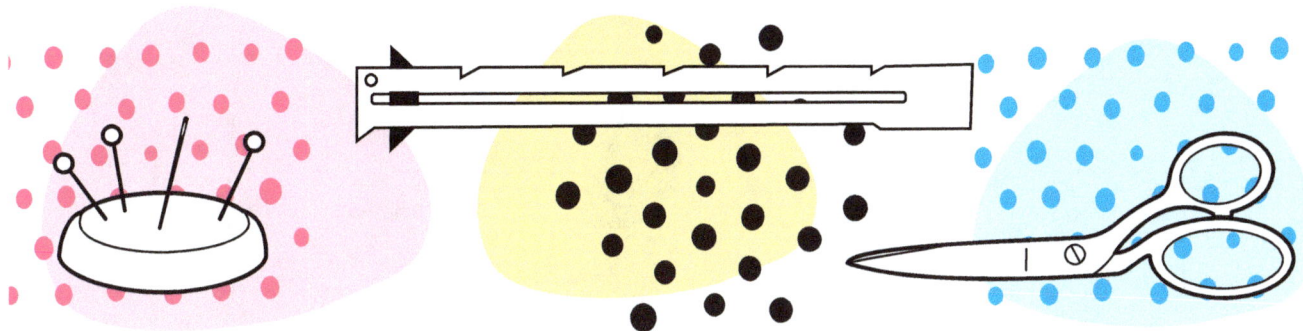

YOKE SKIRT

Use contrasting thread for the skirt's topstitching.

SUPPLIES

Lightweight denim fabric, 1/8 yd (.11m)
3/4" (19mm) wide Velcro® Sleek & Thin™ sew-on tape

Note: PATTERN IS ON PAGE 101. Pattern includes seam allowances. Seam allowances are 1/4" (6mm) unless instructions indicate otherwise.

YOKE SKIRT

1. Staystitch upper edge of YOKE 1/4" (6mm) from raw edge. Clip curves. Press under 1/4" along stitchline. Sew 1/8" (3mm) from pressed edge.

2. To prevent raveling and create a decorative hem finish, sew along lower raw edge of SKIRT with zigzag or overcast stitching.

3. To gather upper edge of skirt, machine baste 1/4" and 1/8" (6mm and 3mm) from raw edge.

4. With RIGHT sides together, pin gathered edge of skirt to lower edge of yoke, arranging gathers to fit. Stitch in place. Press seam up.

5. On OUTSIDE, topstitch yoke close to seamline.

6. With RIGHT sides together, sew up center back of skirt, **1/2" (1.2cm)** from edge, stitching from hem to DOT (see pattern).

7. Apply fasteners; see FINISHING BACK OPENING EDGES, page 9. ♥

3/4 SLEEVE TOP & HAT

SUPPLIES

Lightweight knit fabric, 1/8 yd (.11m)
3/4" (19mm) wide Velcro® Sleek & Thin™ sew-on tape
Felt, 9"x12" (23cm x 30cm) sheet (Hat)
All purpose glue stick, optional

Note: PATTERNS ARE ON PAGE 101. Pattern includes seam allowances. Seam allowances are 1/4" (6mm) unless instructions indicate otherwise.

3/4 SLEEVE TOP

1. With RIGHT sides together, stitch front to back at shoulders.

2. On neckline, machine stitch 1/4" (6mm) from edge. Press or glue* under on stitchline, clipping curves. Sew 1/8" (3mm) from turned edge.
* Note: To glue, lightly dab glue stick along wrong side of seam allowance and finger-press in place.

3. Press under 1/4" (6mm) on ends of sleeves. Sew 1/8" (3mm) from pressed edge.

4. With RIGHT sides together, stitch entire seam of underarms & sides. Clip seam allowance at armpit.

5. Press under 1/4" (6mm) on lower edge of shirt. Sew 1/8" (3mm) from pressed edge.

6. Apply fasteners; see FINISHING BACK OPENING EDGES, page 9, Steps 1-6. ♥

HAT

1. Sew one *long edge* of SIDE to edge of CROWN, 1/8" from edge, with zigzag stitch. Short ends will overlap slightly; sew or glue overlap in place. Turn right side out.

2. Staystitch 1/8" (3mm) from inner curved edge of BRIM.

3. On OUTSIDE of hat, slide brim over top of hat until brim laps 1/8" over SIDE.

4. On INSIDE, hand-sew side to brim with whip stitch, catching edge of side and slipping needle thru staystitching on brim. ♥

RUCHED TOP & 3-TIER SKIRT

SUPPLIES

Lightweight woven cotton fabric, 1/4 yd (.23m)

1/8" wide braided elastic

Note: PATTERNS ARE ON PAGES 103-105. Pattern includes seam allowances. Seam allowances are 1/4" (6mm) unless instructions indicate otherwise.

RUCHED TOP

1. For upper casing, press under 3/4" (2cm) on one long edge. Sew 1/8" and 1/2" (3mm and 1.2cm) from pressed edge.

2. For lower casing, press under 1/2" (1.2cm) on other long edge. Sew 3/8" (9mm) from pressed edge.

3. Cut elastic 4 1/2" (11cm) long. Using a small safety pin, insert elastic thru upper casing and sew securely at ends.

4. Cut elastic 3 1/2" (9cm) long. Using a small safety pin, insert elastic thru lower casing and sew securely at ends.

5. With RIGHT sides together, stitch center back seam. ♥

3-TIER SKIRT

1. For casing, press under 1/2" (1.2cm) on one long edge of TOP TIER. Sew 3/8" (9mm) from pressed edge.

2. To gather MIDDLE TIER, machine baste 1/4" and 1/8" (6mm and 3mm) from one long edge.

3. With RIGHT sides together, pin gathered edge of middle tier to raw edge of TOP TIER, matching centers and having back edges even. Pull up bobbin threads and adjust gathers to fit. Sew in place. Press seam allowance upward. On OUTSIDE, sew top tier close to seam.

4. To connect Part A and Part B of BOTTOM TIER into one long strip, sew the sections RIGHT sides together matching 2 short edges.

5. Press under 1/4" (6mm) hem on one long edge of bottom tier. Sew 1/8" (3mm) from pressed edge.

6. To gather bottom tier, machine baste 1/4" and 1/8" (6mm and 3mm) from long raw edge.

7. With RIGHT sides together, pin gathered edge of bottom tier to raw edge of middle tier, matching centers and having back edges even. Pull up bobbin threads and adjust gathers to fit. Sew in place. Press seam allowance upward. On OUTSIDE, stitch middle tier close to seam.

8. Cut elastic 3 1/2" (9cm) long. Using a small safety pin, insert elastic thru casing and sew securely at ends.

9. With RIGHT sides together, stitch center back seam. ♥

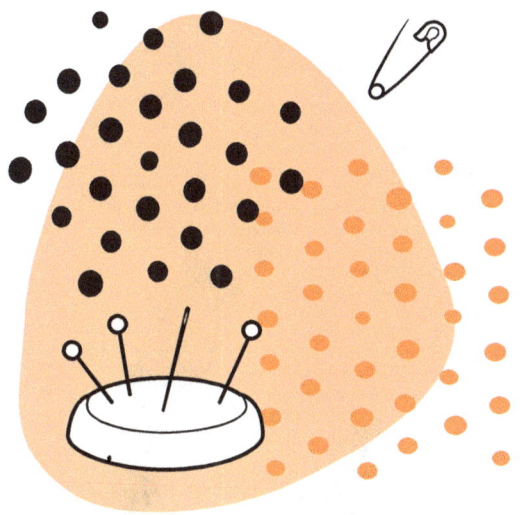

SWING CARDIGAN

The Swing Cardigan is easy to make from a single piece of pre-cut felt. The fuzziness of felt gives the garment a soft, wooley look. I used marbled felt in the pink cardigan pictured.

Step 1 below instructs how to fold the felt before cutting.

SUPPLIES

Felt, 9"x12" (23cm x 30cm) sheet

Note: PATTERN IS ON PAGE 103. Pattern includes seam allowances. Seam allowances are 1/4" (6mm) unless instructions indicate otherwise.

1. Fold the rectangle of felt in half crosswise, then lengthwise. Place pattern on folded edges having shoulder edge on the crosswise folds and center edge on the lengthwise folds. Cut.

2. Unfold as shown below. Cut along dotted line to make front opening and V-shaped neck.

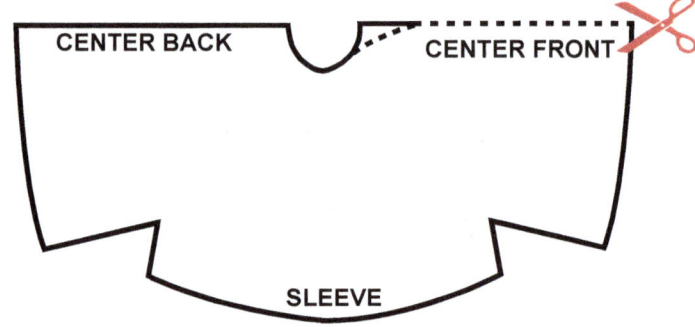

3. Edgestitch 1/8" (3mm) from lower edge of sleeves.

4. Stitch entire underarm seams of jacket and sleeves, pivoting needle at underarm corner. Clip seam allowance at corners. Trim seam allowance to 1/8" (3mm).

5. Edgestitch 1/8" (3mm) from edges along jacket fronts, hemline and neckline. ♥

DENIM JACKET

Use gold thread for the decorative topstitching.

SUPPLIES

Lightweight denim fabric, 1/4 yd (.23m)

3 gold buttons, 1/4" (6mm)

Gold thread

Note: PATTERN IS ON PAGE 63. Pattern includes seam allowances. Seam allowances are 1/4" (6mm) unless instructions indicate otherwise.

1. Sew darts at shoulders. Press darts toward back.

2. With RIGHT sides together, sew FACING to JACKET along front seams and neck edge. Clip neck edge and trim corners. Turn facing to inside and press.

3. Press under **1/2" (1.3cm)** on lower edge of sleeves. Topstitch close to pressed edge. Topstitch again, 1/4" (6mm) from pressed edge.

4. With RIGHT sides together, stitch side seams. Clip underarm curves.

Tip: For a neater appearance, when topstitching Steps 5-6, do not backstitch at the beginning and end of the stitchline. Instead, leave ample excess thread and secure the yarn tails inside garment by hand sewing.

5. Open out facing at lower edge. Press under **1/2" (1.2cm)** hem along entire lower edge of garment and facing. Press facing back in place. Topstitch close to lower edge, catching in facing. Topstitch again, 1/4" (6mm) from lower edge.

6. Topstitch close to front and neck edges. Topstitch again, 1/4" (6mm) from front and neck edges.

7. Sew buttons to one front edge. ♥

POM POM DRESS

SUPPLIES

Lightweight woven cotton fabric, 1/4 yd (.23m) plus small amount of contrasting colors for Ruffle & Straps

1/4" (6mm) wide braided elastic

1/4" (6mm) multicolor craft pom poms

Fabric glue or 3/16" (5mm) permanent glue dots

Note: PATTERN IS ON PAGE 107. Pattern includes seam allowances. Seam allowances are 1/4" (6mm) unless instructions indicate otherwise.

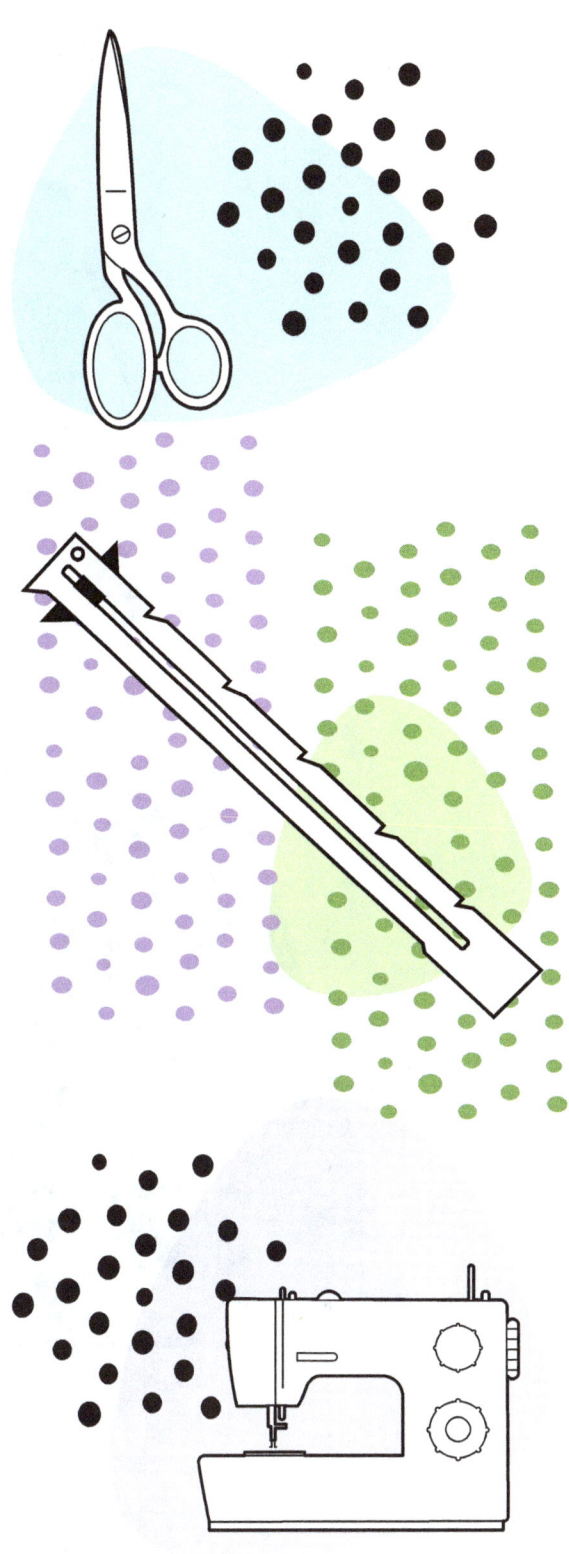

1. Press under 1/4" (6mm) on lower edge of RUFFLE. Sew 1/8" (3mm) from pressed edge.

2. Pin RIGHT side of ruffle to WRONG side of DRESS matching centers and upper edges. Stitch along upper edge. Clip curves.

3. Turn ruffle to OUTSIDE. Press seam. For casing, stitch 3/8" (9mm) from upper edge thru all layers.

4. Cut elastic 5" (12.5cm) long. Using a small safety pin, insert elastic thru casing and tack securely at ends.

5. Press under 1/4" (6mm) on lower edge of dress. Sew 1/8" (3mm) from pressed edge.

6. With RIGHT sides together, stitch center back seam of dress.

7. Press under 1/4" (6mm) on both long edges of STRAPS. Fold straps in half lengthwise, WRONG sides together and press again. Sew 1/8" (3mm) from edge thru all layers.

8. Lapping upper edge of dress 1/4" (6mm) over straps, sew front of straps 1/2" from center front and back of straps 1/2" from center back, being careful not to twist straps.

9. Glue POM POMS to dress as pictured. ♥

FLARED MAXI SKIRT & CAMISOLE

The pieces of this set are very versatile to mix and match with other tops and bottoms.

For a simple variation, cut the camisole 1/4" longer to cover the doll's midriff.

Pictured with Trapezoid Purse, page 23.

SUPPLIES

Lightweight woven cotton fabric, 1/4 yd (.23m)
3/4" (19mm) wide Velcro® Sleek & Thin™ sew-on tape
1/4" (6mm) wide braided elastic

Note: PATTERN IS ON PAGE 109. Pattern includes seam allowances. Seam allowances are 1/4" (6mm) unless instructions indicate otherwise.

SKIRT

1. With RIGHT sides together, stitch SKIRT front to back at side seams.

2. To make casing, press under 1/2" (1.2cm) at upper edge. Sew 3/8" (1cm) from pressed edge, leaving an opening to insert elastic.

3. Cut elastic 3 1/2" (9cm) long. Using a small safety pin, insert elastic thru casing. Overlap ends 1/4" (6mm) and sew securely.

4. Sew opening in casing with a few running stitches by hand.

5. Press under 1/4" (6mm) hem on lower edge of skirt. Sew 1/8" (3mm) from pressed edge. ♥

CAMISOLE

1. Sew darts in CAMISOLE. Press darts toward center.

2. Press under 1/4" (6mm) on upper and lower edges of camisole. Sew 1/8" (3mm) from pressed edges.

3. Press under 1/4" (6mm) on both long edges of STRAPS. Fold straps in half lengthwise, WRONG sides together and press again. Sew lengthwise along center of strap thru all layers.

4. Lap upper edge of camisole 1/4" (6mm) over ends of straps at DOTS (see pattern) using care not to twist straps. Sew straps in place.

5. Apply fasteners; see FINISHING BACK OPENING EDGES, page 9, Steps 1-6. ♥

STARSHINE JUMPSUIT & SPATS

Refer to the photos and plan your cutting carefully to get contrasting colors on the jumpsuit as pictured. The color of the bodice fronts and backs should match at the shoulder seams.

To press metallic fabric, use a low iron temperature and a press cloth. Test on scraps of fabric first.

The spats are open at the bottom to be worn over doll shoes for the look of boots. Try making them in assorted colors to spice up any outfit!

SUPPLIES

Metallic stretch knit, 1/8 yd (.11m) of 2 colors

10mm star plastic gems

3/4" (19mm) wide Velcro® Sleek & Thin™ sew-on tape

1 snap

Fabric glue

3/16" (.5cm) super strength mini glue dots or Aleene's Jewel-It embellishing glue

Note: PATTERNS ARE ON PAGE 111. Pattern includes seam allowances. Seam allowances are 1/4" (6mm) unless instructions indicate otherwise.

JUMPSUIT

1. With RIGHT sides together, stitch BODICE FRONT sections together at center front.

2. With RIGHT sides together, stitch BODICE FRONT to BODICE BACKS at shoulder seams including facing sections. Clip seams at curve.

3. Turn facing to inside along foldline at neck edge. Glue in place.

4. Turn under 1/4" (6mm) hem on lower edge of sleeves. Sew 1/8" (3mm) from turned edge.

5. With RIGHT sides together, stitch underarm seams. Clip curves.

6. With RIGHT sides together, stitch center front seam of PANTS. Clip curves.

7. Turn under 1/4" (6mm) hem on lower edges of pants. Sew 1/8" (3mm) from turned edge.

8. With RIGHT sides together, pin pants to bodice at waistline seam, matching center fronts and back edges. Stitch in place. Turn seam toward bodice and tack in place with glue.

9. With RIGHT sides together, sew center back seam of pants, **1/2" (1.2cm)** from edge, stitching from crotch to DOT (see pattern). Clip curve.

10. With RIGHT sides together, sew front to back of pants at inner leg seams, matching center seams.

11. Apply fasteners; see FINISHING BACK OPENING EDGES, page 9.

12. On BELT, glue under 1/4" (6mm) on both long edges. Fold belt in half lengthwise, WRONG SIDES TOGETHER. Sew along center of belt thru all layers.

13. Sew snap to ends of belt.

14. Using glue dots or embellishing glue, attach a star gem to center front of belt. Attach another star gem to one side of bodice, positioned 1/2" (1.2cm) from shoulder seam and 1/2" (1.2cm) from center front seam. ♥

SPATS

1. Turn under 1/4" (6mm) on upper edge of each spat. Sew 1/8" (3mm) from turned edge.

2. With RIGHT sides together, sew center front seam, 1/8" (3mm) from edge, from top to toe. Trim seam allowance at an angle at each end. ♥

SIMPLE DRESS

This simple style features a fitted bodice and a slightly gathered skirt. So cute with boots!

SUPPLIES

Lightweight woven or knit cotton fabric, 1/8 yd (.11m)
3/4" (19mm) wide Velcro® Sleek & Thin™ sew-on tape
All purpose glue stick, optional

Note: PATTERN IS ON PAGE 113. Pattern includes seam allowances. Seam allowances are 1/4" (6mm) unless instructions indicate otherwise.

1. Sew darts in BODICE FRONT. Press darts toward center.

2. With RIGHT sides together, stitch BODICE FRONT to BODICE BACK at shoulders.

3. On neckline, machine stitch 1/4" (6mm) from edge. Press or glue* under on stitchline, clipping curves. Sew 1/8" (3mm) from turned edge.
* Note: To glue, lightly dab glue stick along wrong side of seam allowance and finger-press in place.

4. On armholes, machine stitch 1/4" (6mm) from edge. Clip curves at close intervals.

5. To ease top of sleeve, machine baste 1/4" and 1/8" (6mm and 3mm) from raw edge.

6. With RIGHT sides together, pin sleeves to armhole edge of bodice, matching DOT (see pattern) to shoulder seam and pulling up ease stitches to fit. Sew in place. Trim seam allowance and press it toward sleeve.

7. Press under 1/4" (6mm) on lower edge of SLEEVES. Sew 1/8" from pressed edge.

8. With RIGHT sides together, sew front to back at entire underarm seams, matching the armhole seams.

9. Press under 1/4" (6mm) on lower edge of SKIRT. Sew 1/8" (3mm) from pressed edge.

10. To gather upper edge of skirt, machine baste 1/4" and 1/8" (6mm and 3mm) from raw edge.

11. With RIGHT sides together, pin skirt to bodice at waistline seam, matching centers and having back edges even. Pull up bobbin threads and adjust gathers to fit. Sew in place. Press seam allowance toward bodice.

12. On OUTSIDE, topstitch bodice close to waistline seam.

13. With RIGHT sides together, sew up center back of skirt, **1/2" (1.2cm** from edge, stitching from hem to DOT (see pattern).

14. Apply fasteners; see FINISHING BACK OPENING EDGES, page 9. ♥

BABYDOLL DRESS

This empire-waist style features a self-fabric bow. The fabric for my dress was upcycled from a womens' blouse.

SUPPLIES

Lightweight woven fabric, 1/4 yd (.23m)
3/4" (19mm) wide Velcro® Sleek & Thin™ sew-on tape
Fabric glue, optional

Note: PATTERN IS ON PAGE 115. Pattern includes seam allowances. Seam allowances are 1/4" (6mm) unless instructions indicate otherwise.

1. To staystitch BODICE, sew 1/4" (6mm) from upper edge. Press under 1/4" (6mm) using the stitchline for a guide, clipping to staystitching at center front. Sew 1/8" (3mm) from pressed edge.

2. Press under 1/4" (6mm) hem on lower edge of SKIRT. Sew 1/8" (3mm) from pressed edge.

3. To gather skirt, machine baste 1/4" and 1/8" (6mm and 3mm) from upper edge.

4. With RIGHT sides together, pin skirt to bodice at waistline seam, matching centers and pulling up bobbin threads to fit. Stitch in place. Press seam allowance toward bodice.

5. On STRAPS, press under 1/8" (3mm) on long edges. Fold in half lengthwise, WRONG sides together, and press again. Sew lengthwise along middle of straps thru all layers.

6. Lap upper edge of bodice 1/4" (6mm) over straps at DOTS (see pattern), being careful not to twist straps. Sew straps in place.

7. On BOW, press under 1/4" (6mm) on sides A and B. With RIGHT sides together, fold piece in half so that pressed edges meet. Sew across raw edges C and D. Trim seam allowance and clip corners. Turn right side out. Gather across center. Pull gathers tight and secure with a knot.

8. On BOW CENTER, press under 1/8" (3mm) on long edges. Fold in half lengthwise, WRONG sides together, and press again. Wrap around middle of bow. Secure in place with hand sewing or glue.

9. With RIGHT sides together, fold BOW TAIL in half lengthwise. Sew 1/4" (6mm) from long edges to make a tube. Trim seam allowance. Using a small safety pin or loop turner (see Page 7), turn right side out. Tuck raw ends inside and secure openings with glue, or hand-sewing with slip stitch.

10. Fold bow tail in half to make an inverted V. Stack bow on top of tails at center front of bodice. Sew or glue in place.

11. Sew up center back of dress, **1/2" (1.2cm)** from edge, stitching from hem to DOT (see pattern).

12. Apply fasteners; see FINISHING BACK OPENING EDGES, page 9. ♥

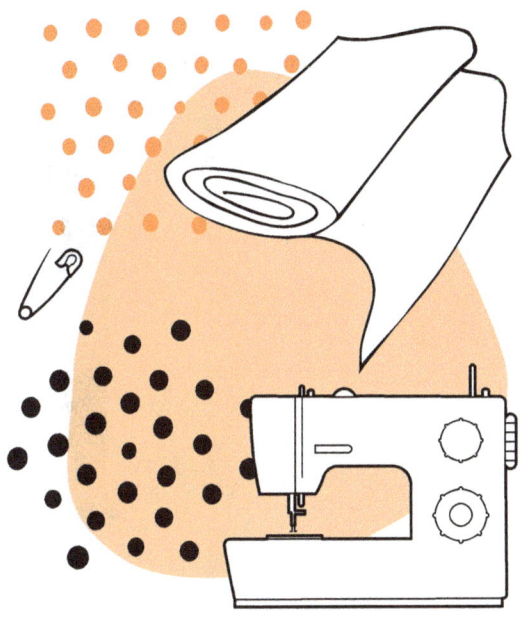

NIGHTGOWN

SUPPLIES

Lightweight woven cotton fabric, 1/4 yd (.23m)

1/8" (3mm) wide satin ribbon

Note: PATTERN IS ON PAGE 117. Pattern includes seam allowances. Seam allowances are 1/4" (6mm) unless instructions indicate otherwise.

1. With RIGHT sides together, stitch center front seam of nightgown front sections, **leaving a gap between dots** for drawstring (see dots on pattern). Press seam open. Topstitch 1/8" (3mm) from each side of seam.

2. Sew 1/4" (6mm) from all raw armhole edges. Clip curves. Press to inside on stitching lines. Sew 1/8" (3mm) from pressed edges.

3. For casing, press under 1/2" (1.2cm) along neckline edges of front and back sections. Sew 3/8" (8mm) from pressed edges.

4. With RIGHT sides together, stitch front to back at side seams.

5. Press under 1/4" (6mm) hem on lower edge. Sew 1/8" (3mm) from pressed edge.

6. Cut an 18" (46cm) piece of ribbon. Starting & ending at center front, using a small safety pin, insert ribbon thru neckline casings having ends extend evenly.

7. Gather neckline with drawstring to fit doll and tie ribbon tails in a bow. ♥

BATHROBE

This pattern uses a quarter-fold method of fabric cutting for less seams to sew. See Steps 1-2 below.

SUPPLIES

Piece of cotton flannel fabric, 10"x18" (25x46cm)

5/8" (15mm) wide satin ribbon

Note: PATTERN IS ON PAGE 119. Pattern includes seam allowances. Seam allowances are 1/4" (6mm) unless instructions indicate otherwise.

1. Fold fabric in half crosswise, then lengthwise.

2. Lay edges of PATTERN on folded edges of fabric, having shoulder edge on crosswise folds and center edge on lengthwise folds. Cut out.

3. Refold fabric as shown in Fig. A. Referring to dashed line on Fig. A, cut apart along **CENTER FRONT** to make robe opening and taper near neckline to create V-neck.

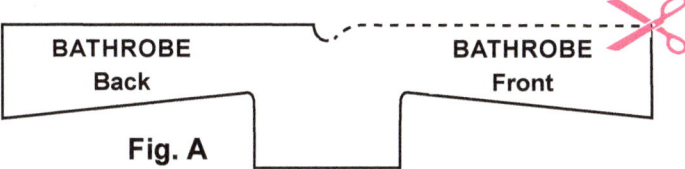

Fig. A

4. For BINDING, press 1 yd (1m) of ribbon in half lengthwise. Clip neck curve of robe. Encase front, neck and sleeve edges with ribbon, sewing thru all thicknesses.

5. With RIGHT sides together, sew entire underarm seams of robe and sleeves. Clip underarm curves.

6. Press under 1/2" (1.2cm) hem at bottom of robe, mitering front corners. Sew 3/8" (8mm) from pressed edge.

7. For BELT, cut a piece of ribbon 14" (36cm) long. Press in half lengthwise. Sew lengthwise edges together. To prevent fraying, apply a tiny bit of clear glue along ends. Mark center of belt and tack to center back of robe, on waistline, if desired. ♥

HOSIERY

Colorful hosiery is a fun way to elevate an outfit. It's also easy to make. Upcycle old tights, socks, and t-shirts — or purchase ornamental fabric such as stretch lace. Be sure to use a ballpoint needle or stretch needle in your sewing machine to sew smoothly and avoid snags. To maintain stretch in the fabric, use a short, narrow zigzag stitch. If you have trouble fitting your doll shoes over hosiery, cut a slit down the back of the shoes with scissors.

TIGHTS

SUPPLIES

Stretch knit fabric

1/4" (6mm) wide braided elastic

Ballpoint or stretch needle

Note: PATTERN IS ON PAGE 121. Pattern includes seam allowances. Seam allowances are 1/4" (6mm) unless instructions indicate otherwise.

1. With RIGHT sides together, stitch center front seam using zigzag at a *short narrow* setting. Trim seam allowance to 1/8" (3mm).

2. For casing, press under 1/2" (1.2cm) at upper edge. Stitch over raw edge using zigag at a *long wide* setting. *By overlapping your zigzag stitches over the raw edge, this will prevent the fabric from rolling and keep it laying flat.*

3. Cut elastic 4 1/4" (10.5cm) long. Using a small safety pin, insert elastic thru casing and sew securely at ends.

4. With RIGHT sides together, stitch center back seam using zigzag at a *short narrow* setting. Trim seam allowance to 1/8" (3mm).

5. With RIGHT sides together, pin inner leg seam matching raw edges and aligning center seams at crotch. Stitch from toe-to-toe using zigzag at a *short narrow* setting. Trim seam allowance to 1/8" (3mm). Turn right-side out with long tweezers (see Page 7). ♥

THIGH HIGH STOCKINGS

SUPPLIES

Stretch knit fabric

Ballpoint or stretch needle

Note: PATTERN IS ON PAGE 121. Pattern includes seam allowances. Seam allowances are 1/4" (6mm) unless instructions indicate otherwise.

1. Press under 1/4" (6mm) on upper edge. Stitch over raw edge using zigag at a *long wide* setting. *By overlapping your zigzag stitches over the raw edge, this will prevent the fabric from rolling and keep it laying flat.*

2. Fold stocking in half lengthwise with RIGHT sides together. Pin together along raw edges. Stitch using zigag at a *short narrow* setting. Trim seam allowance to 1/8" (3mm). Turn right-side out with long tweezers (see Page 7). ♥

SOCKS

SUPPLIES

Stretch knit fabric

Ballpoint or stretch needle

Note: PATTERN IS ON PAGE 121. Pattern includes seam allowances. Seam allowances are 1/4" (6mm) unless instructions indicate otherwise.

1. Press under 1/4" (6mm) on upper edge. Stitch over raw edge using zigag at a *long wide* setting. *By overlapping your zigzag stitches over the raw edge, this will prevent the fabric from rolling and keep it laying flat.*

2. Fold socks in half lengthwise with RIGHT sides together. Pin together along raw edges. Stitch using zigag at a *short narrow* setting. Trim seam allowance to 1/8" (3mm). Turn right-side out with long tweezers (see Page 7). ♥

APRON

The Apron is pictured with T-Shirt, Page 19 and Leggings, Page 25.

SUPPLIES

Lightweight woven cotton fabric, 1/8 yd (.11m)
5/8" (1.5cm) wide satin ribbon
3/4" (19mm) wide Velcro® Sleek & Thin™ sew-on tape
Fabric glue

Note: PATTERN IS ON PAGE 123. Pattern includes seam allowances. Seam allowances are 1/4" (6mm) unless instructions indicate otherwise.

1. Press under 1/4" (6mm) hem on lower edge of SKIRT. Sew 1/8" (3mm) from pressed edge.

2. Press under 1/4" (6mm) on side edges of skirt. Sew 1/8" (3mm) from pressed edges.

3. To gather upper edge of skirt, machine baste 1/4" and 1/8" (6mm and 3mm) from raw edge.

4. On OUTSIDE, lap and pin lower edge of WAISTBAND 1/4" (6mm) over upper edge of skirt, between dots (see pattern), matching center fronts. Pull up gathers and adjust to fit. Sew close to edge of waistband.

5. With RIGHT sides together, fold BIB in half crosswise. Sew along side edges. Trim corners, turn right-side out and press. Topstitch 1/8" (3mm) from edge along sides and top.

6. On OUTSIDE, pin upper edge of waistband 1/4" (6mm) over lower edge of bib, matching center fronts. Sew close to edge of waistband.

7. Turn in ends of waistband 1/4" (6mm). Press. Sew or glue to secure turned ends.

8. Press under 1/4" (6mm) on both long edges of STRAPS. Press in half lengthwise, WRONG sides together. Sew 1/8" (3mm) from edge thru all layers.

9. Lap front end of each strap 1/4" (6mm) under top edge of bib, aligning outer edge of strap with outer edge of bib. Sew or glue in place.

10. Lap back end of each strap 1/4" (6mm) under top edge of waistband and 1" from back of waistband. Sew or glue in place.

11. Cut patches of Velcro for closures at ends of waistband and glue in place. ♥

FULL-SIZE PATTERNS

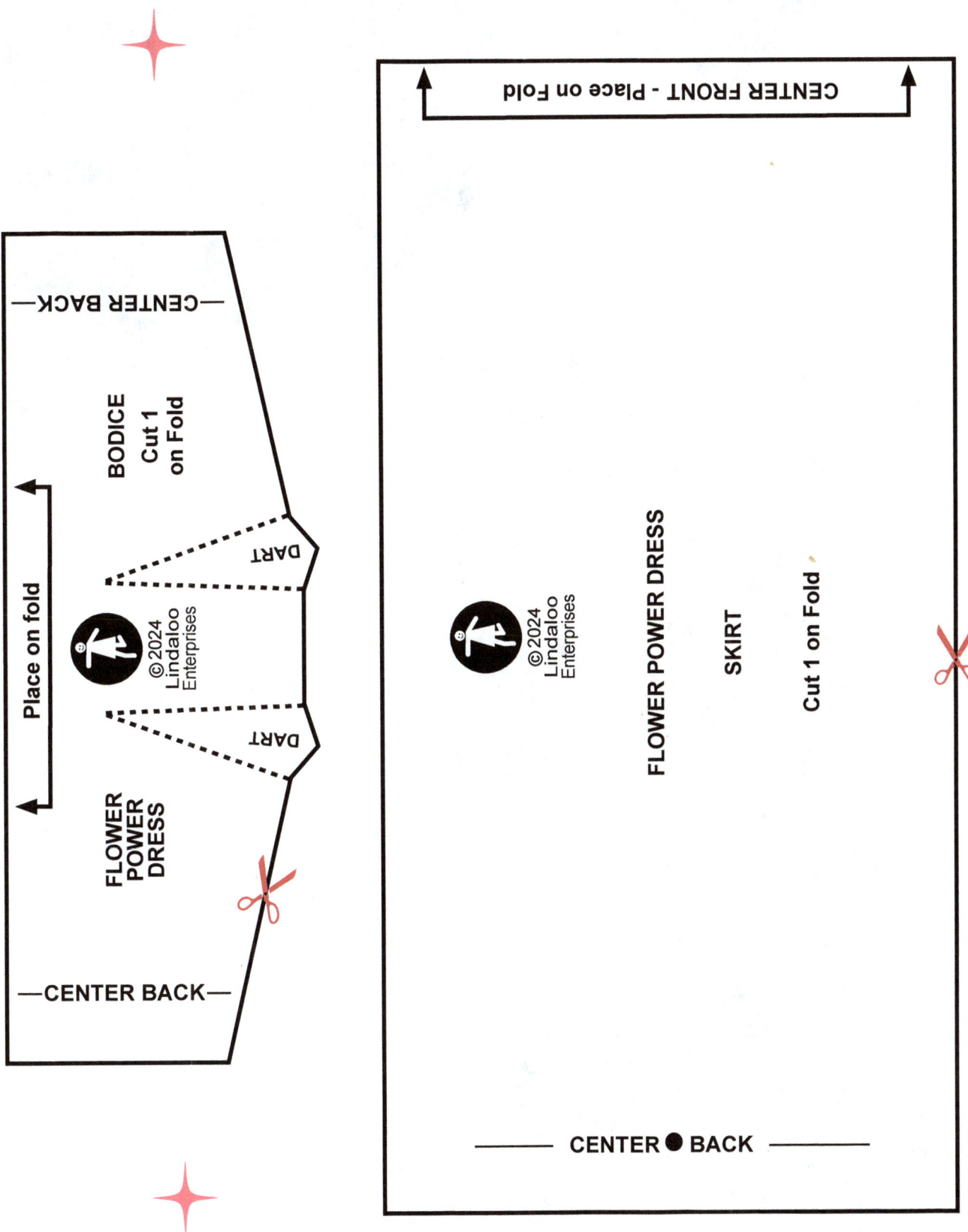

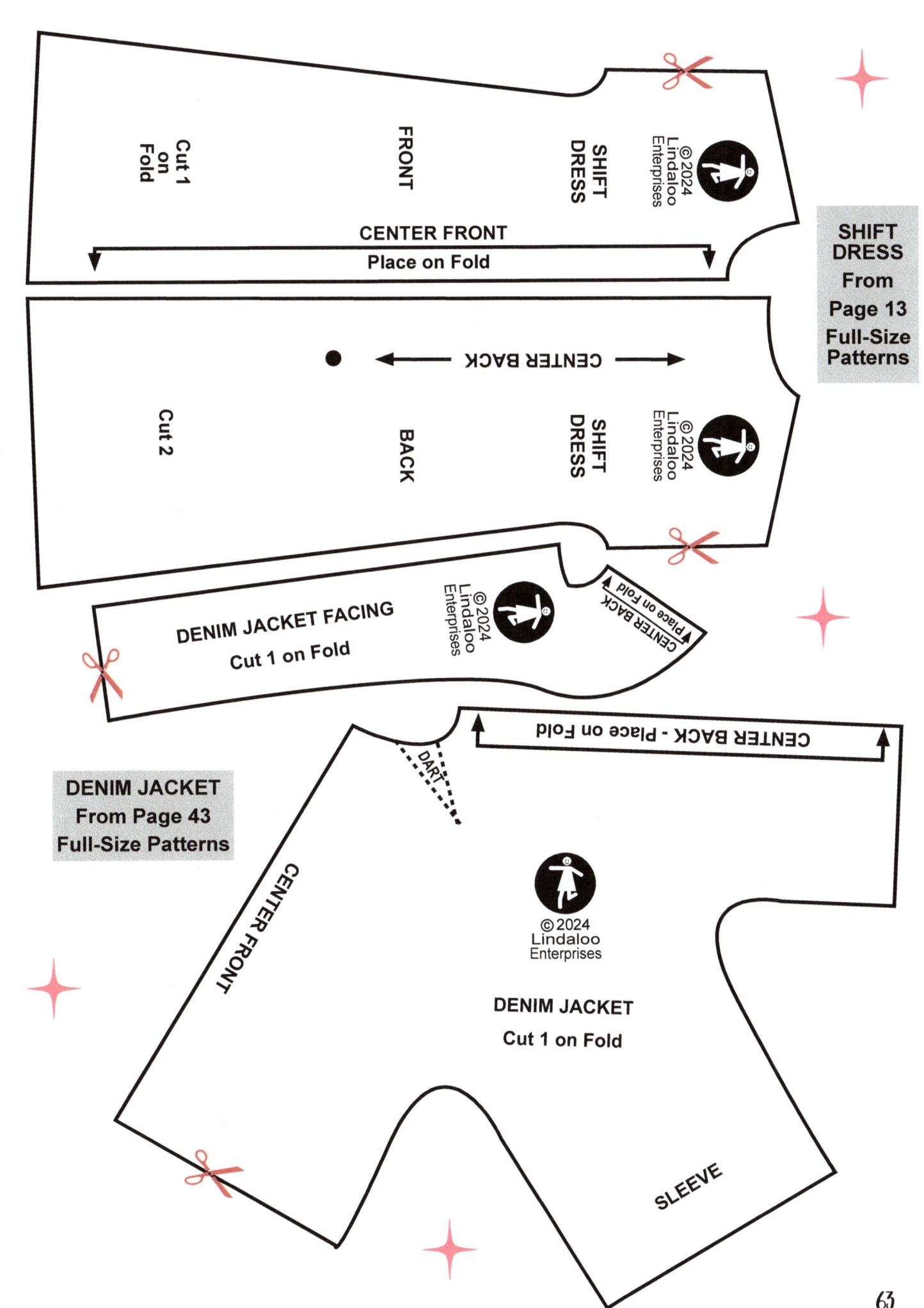

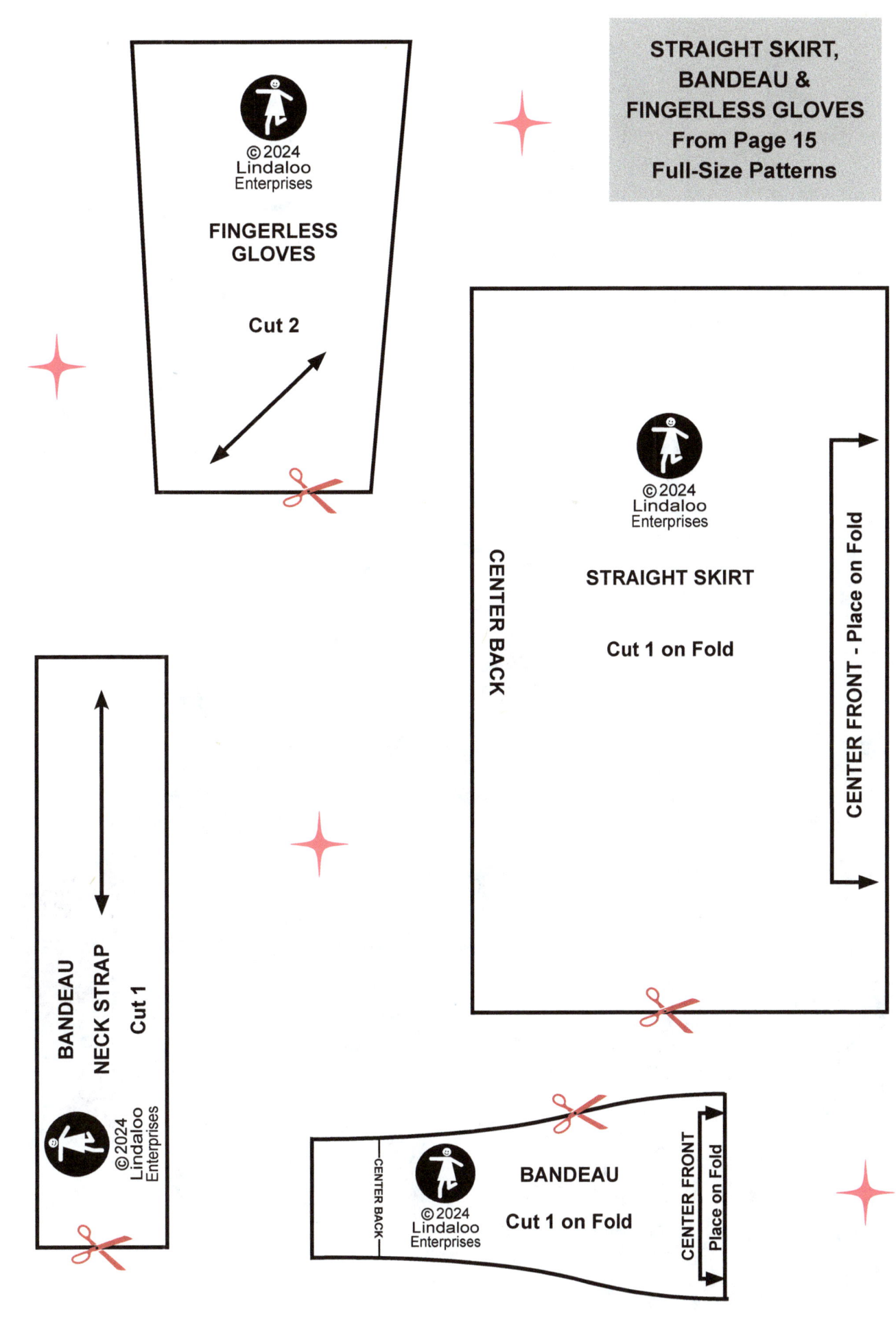

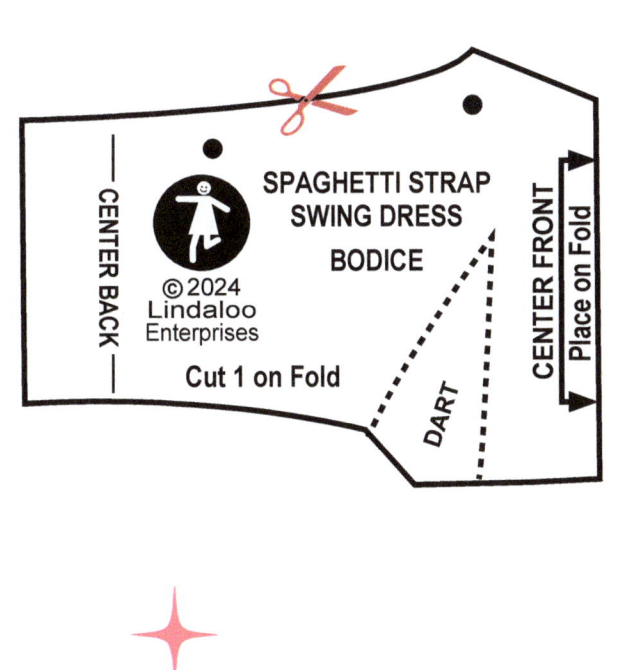
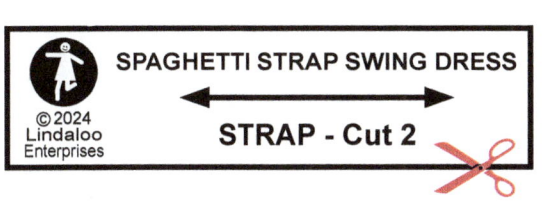

**PART 1
SPAGHETTI STRAP
SWING DRESS**
From Page 17
Full-Size Patterns

Note:
Tape Part 1 and Part 2 of Skirt pattern together before cutting fabric.

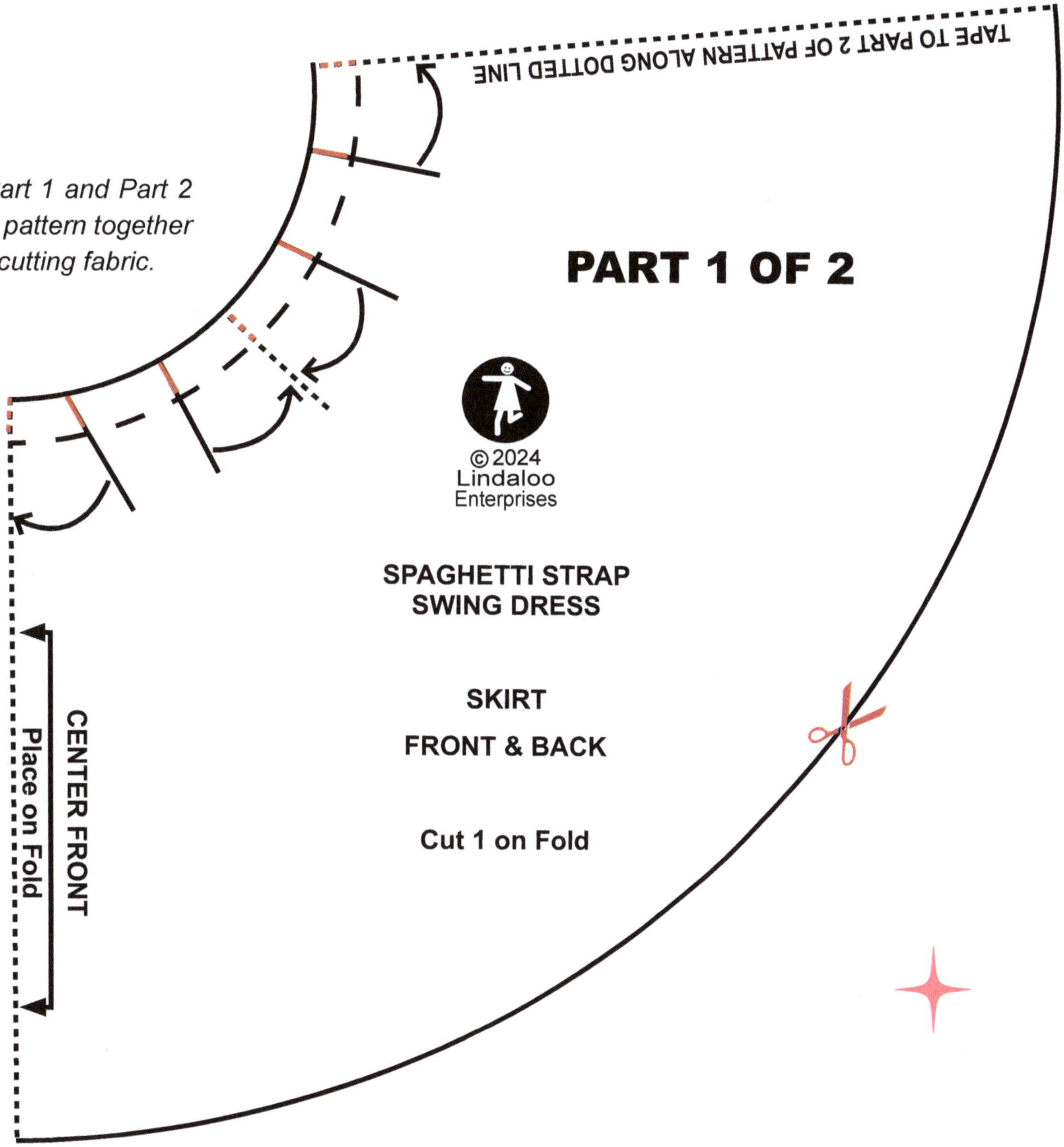

PART 1 OF 2

SPAGHETTI STRAP SWING DRESS

SKIRT

FRONT & BACK

Cut 1 on Fold

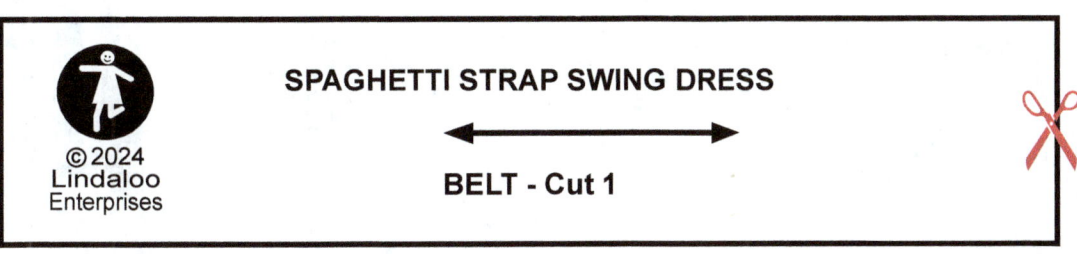

PART 2
SPAGHETTI STRAP
SWING DRESS
From Page 17
Full-Size Patterns

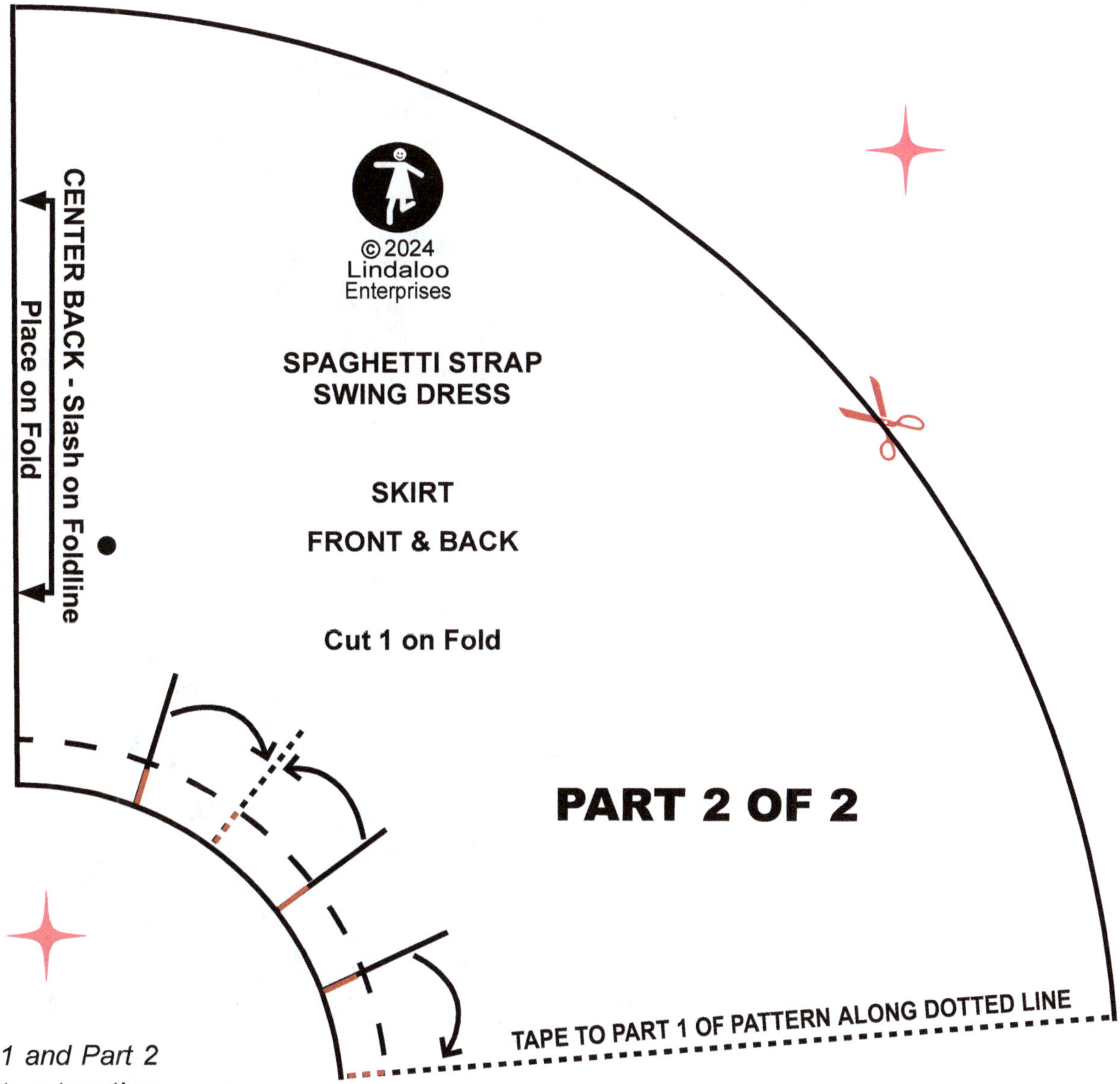

SPAGHETTI STRAP SWING DRESS

© 2024 Lindaloo Enterprises

← →

BELT - Cut 1

SPAGHETTI STRAP SWING DRESS

© 2024 Lindaloo Enterprises

CENTER BACK - Slash on Foldline
Place on Fold

SKIRT
FRONT & BACK

Cut 1 on Fold

PART 2 OF 2

TAPE TO PART 1 OF PATTERN ALONG DOTTED LINE

Note:
Tape Part 1 and Part 2 of Skirt pattern together before cutting fabric.

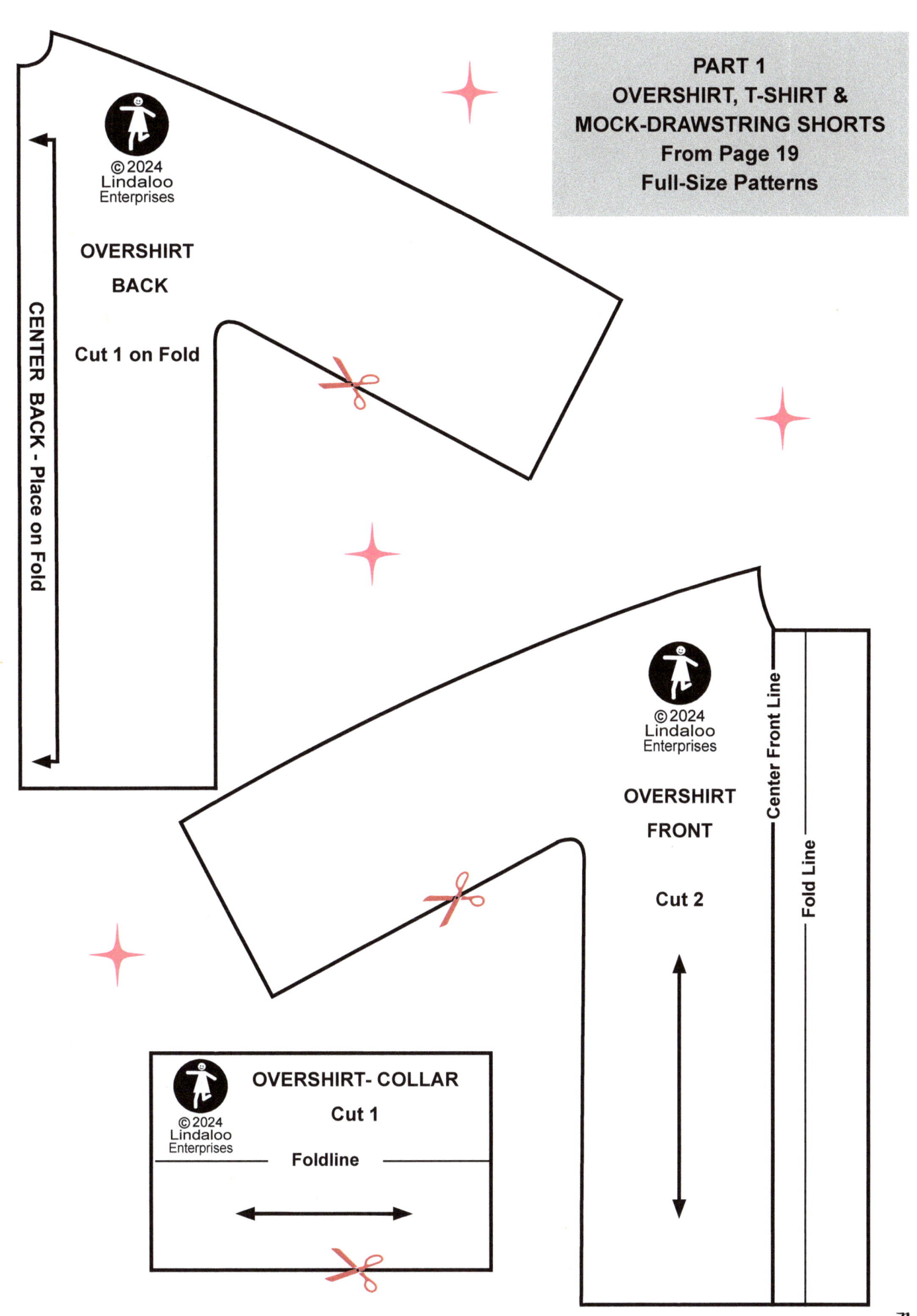

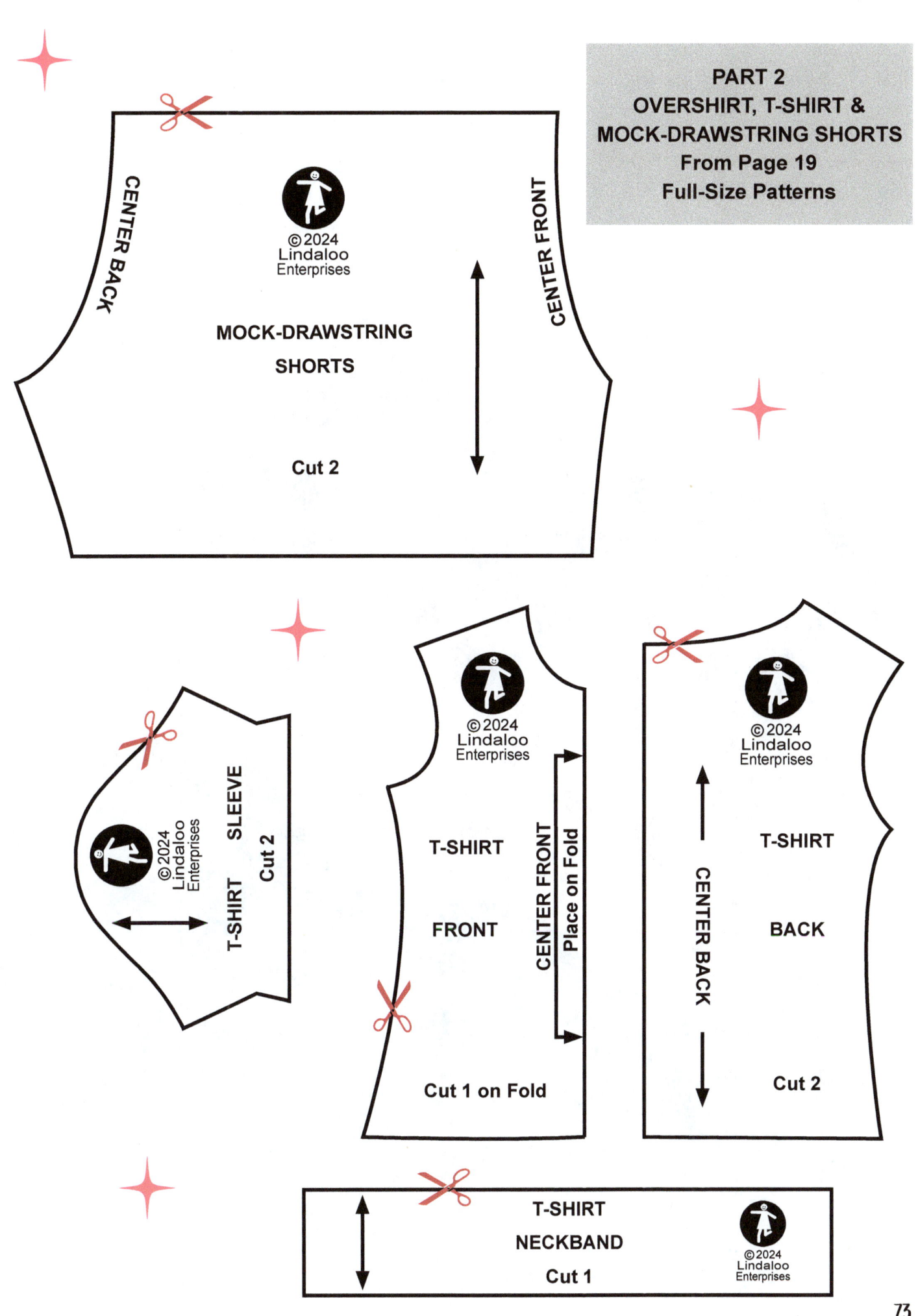

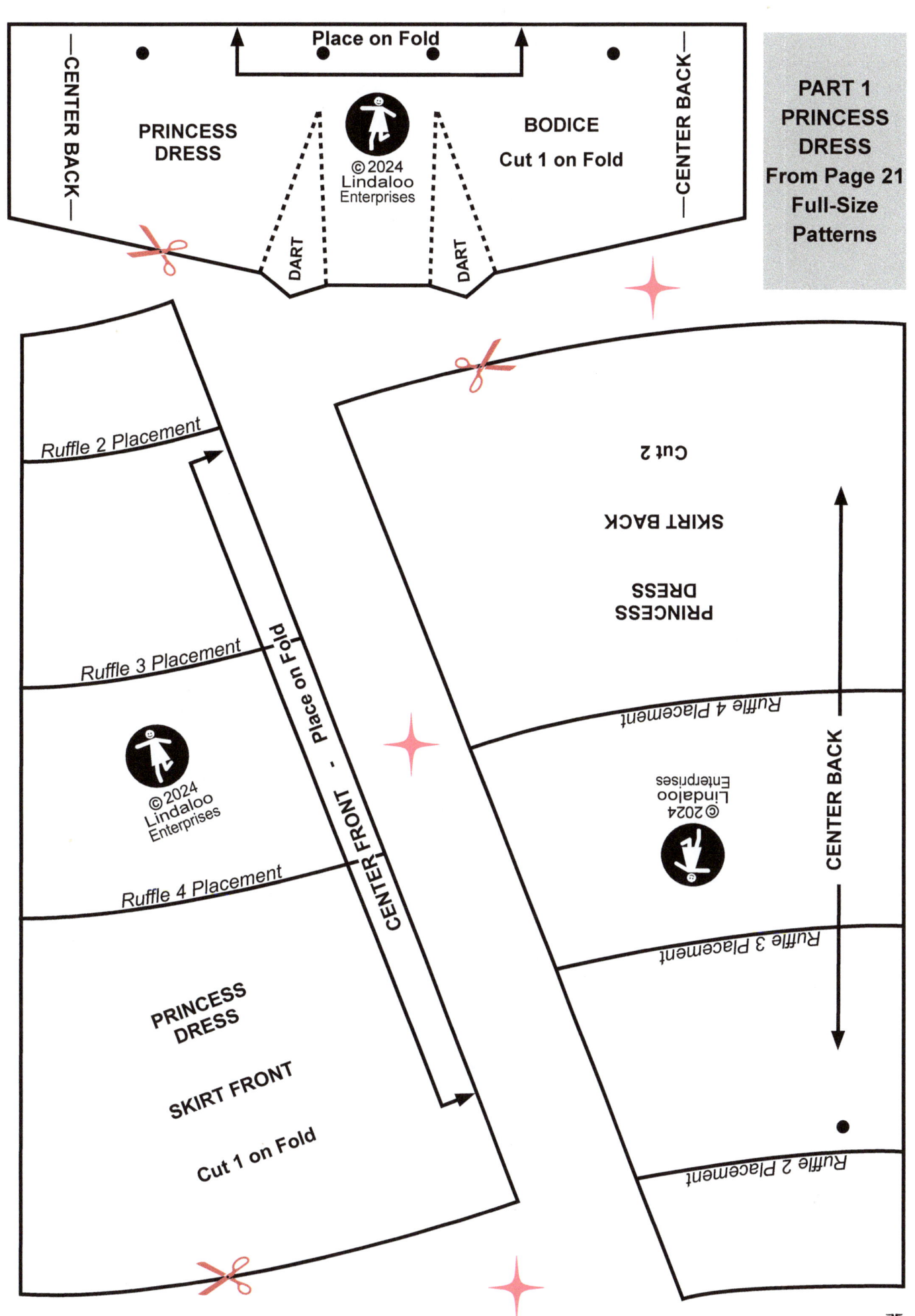

**PART 2
PRINCESS
DRESS
From Page 21
Full-Size
Patterns**

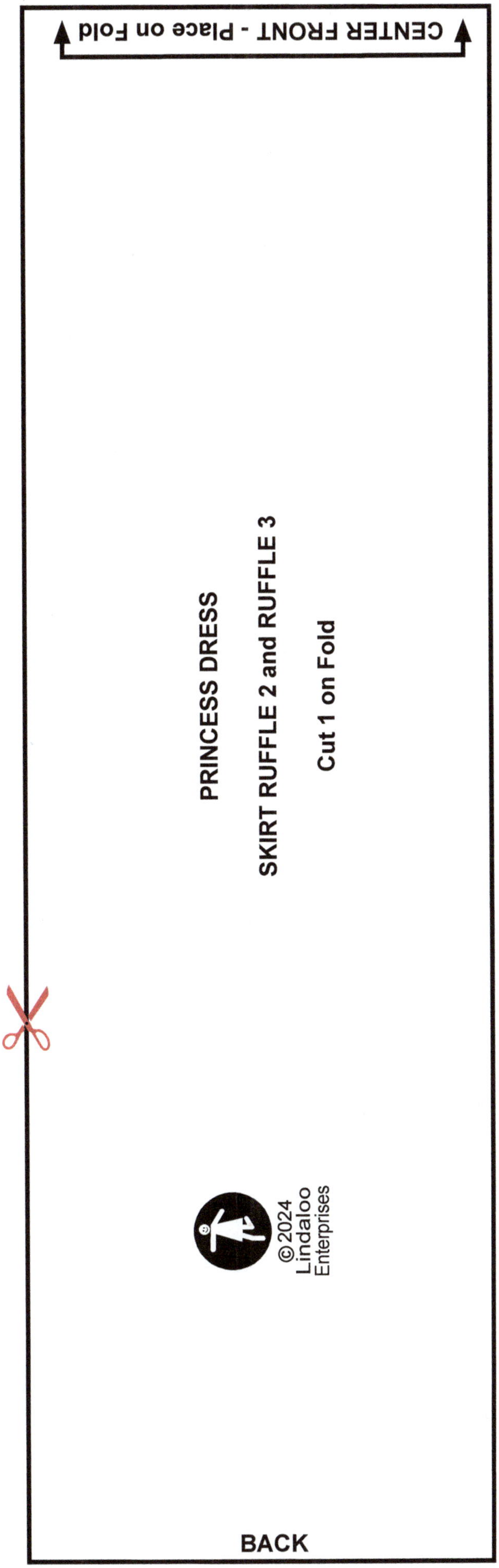

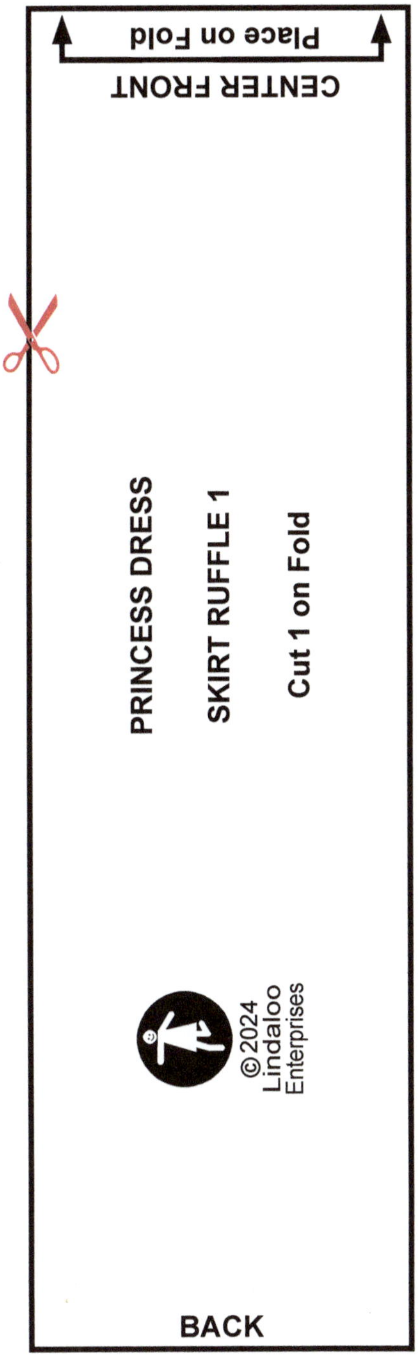

↑ CENTER FRONT - Place on Fold ↑

PRINCESS DRESS

SKIRT RUFFLE 2 and RUFFLE 3

Cut 1 on Fold

© 2024 Lindaloo Enterprises

BACK

↑ CENTER FRONT
Place on Fold ↑

PRINCESS DRESS

SKIRT RUFFLE 1

Cut 1 on Fold

© 2024 Lindaloo Enterprises

BACK

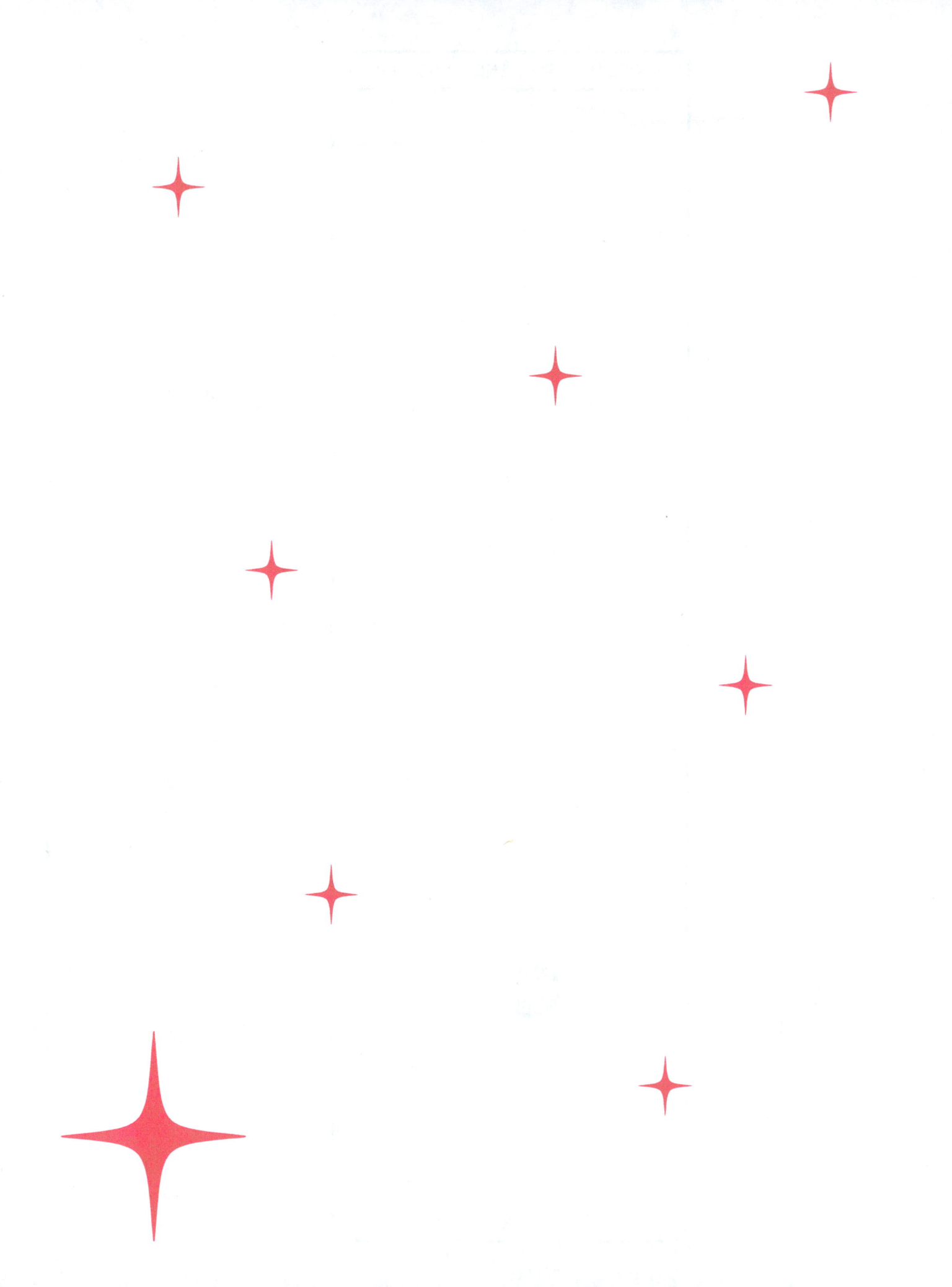

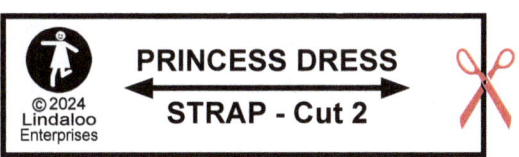

PART 3
PRINCESS DRESS
From Page 21
Full-Size Patterns

Pattern for **Ruffle 4** is in 2 sections. Tape Part A to Part B before cutting fabric.

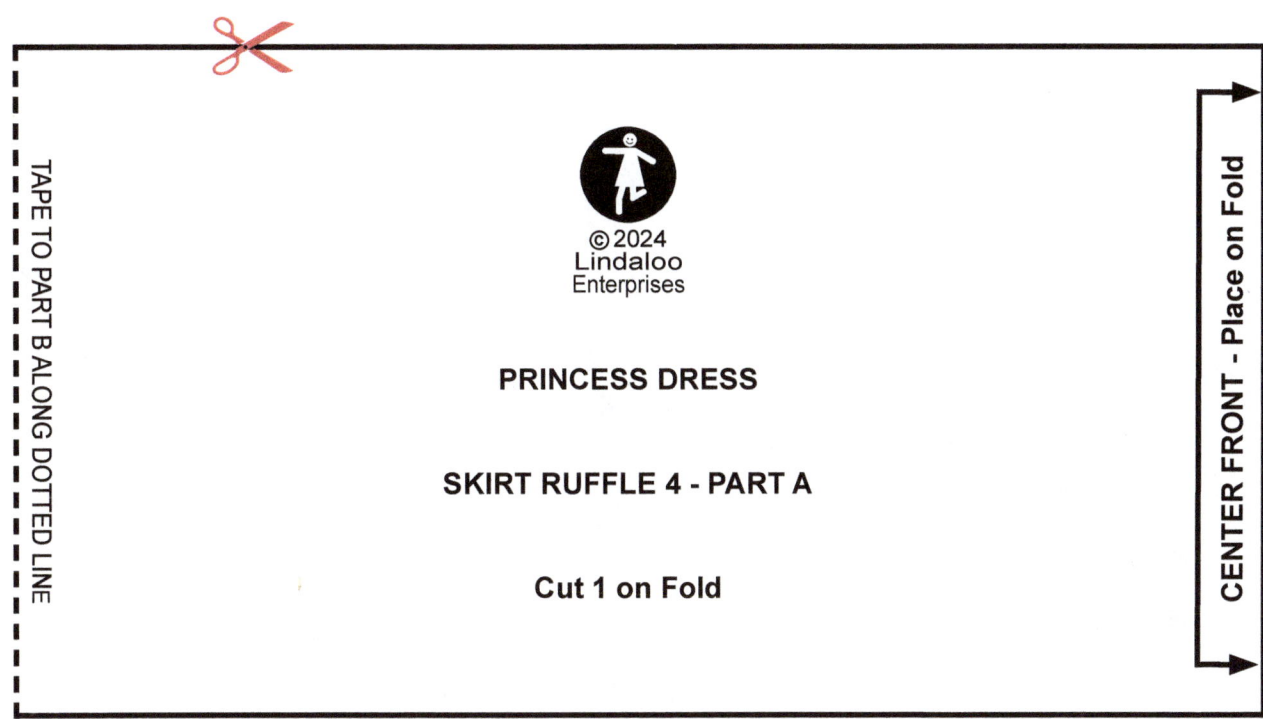

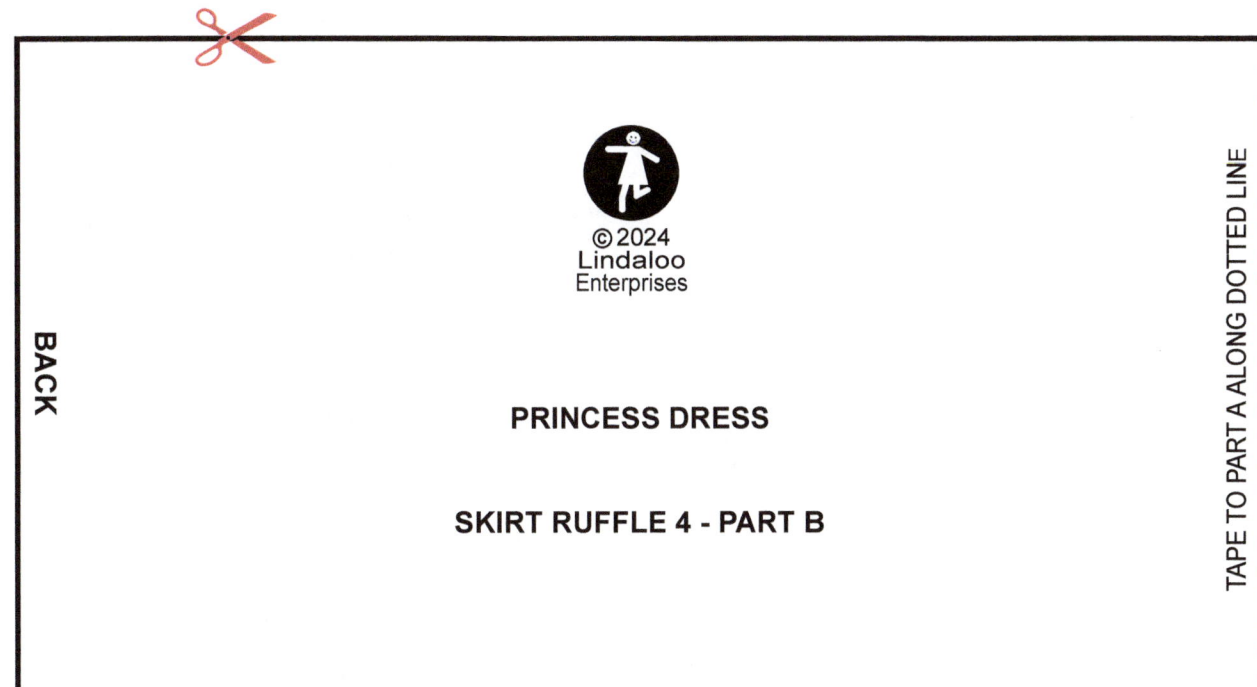

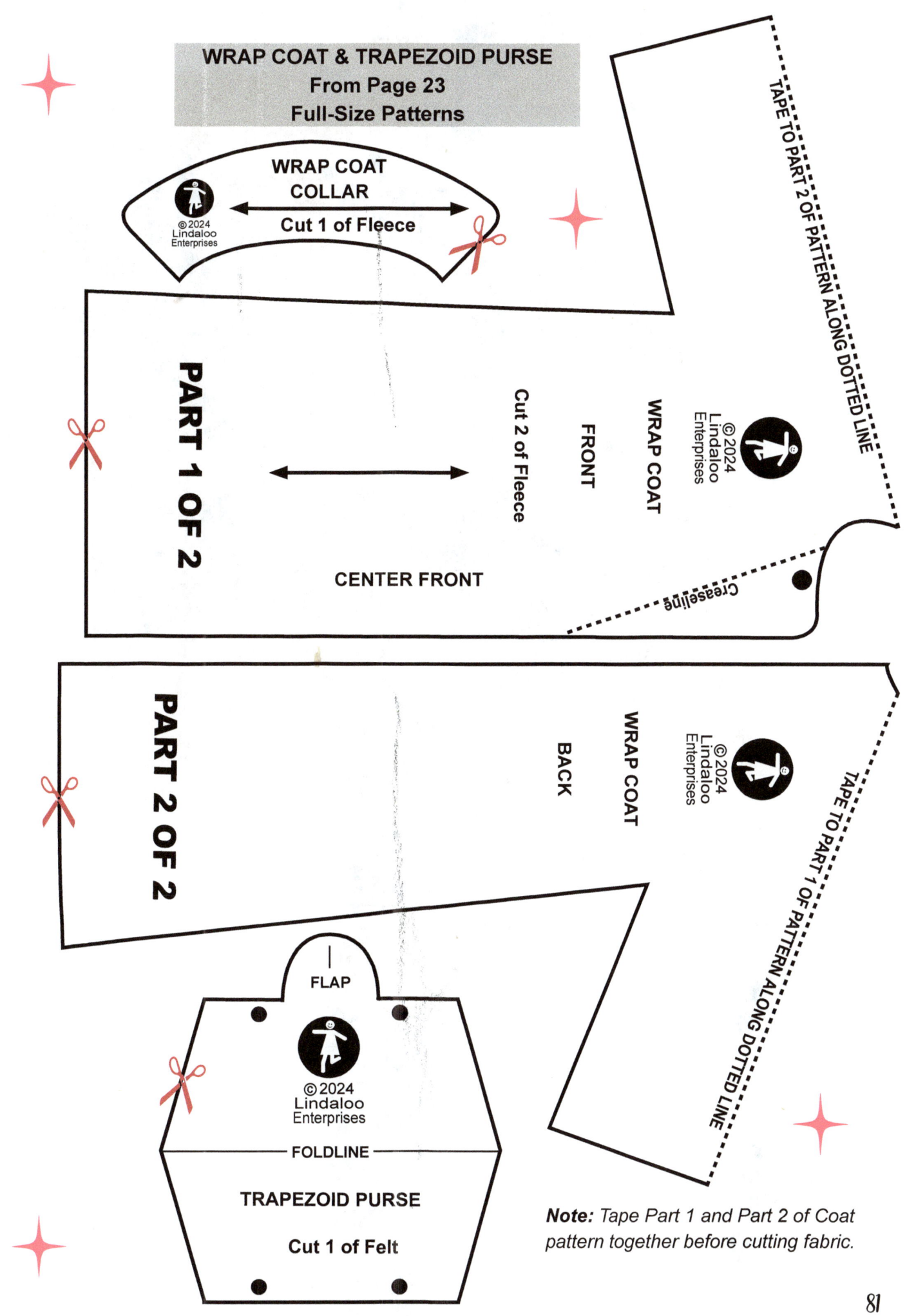

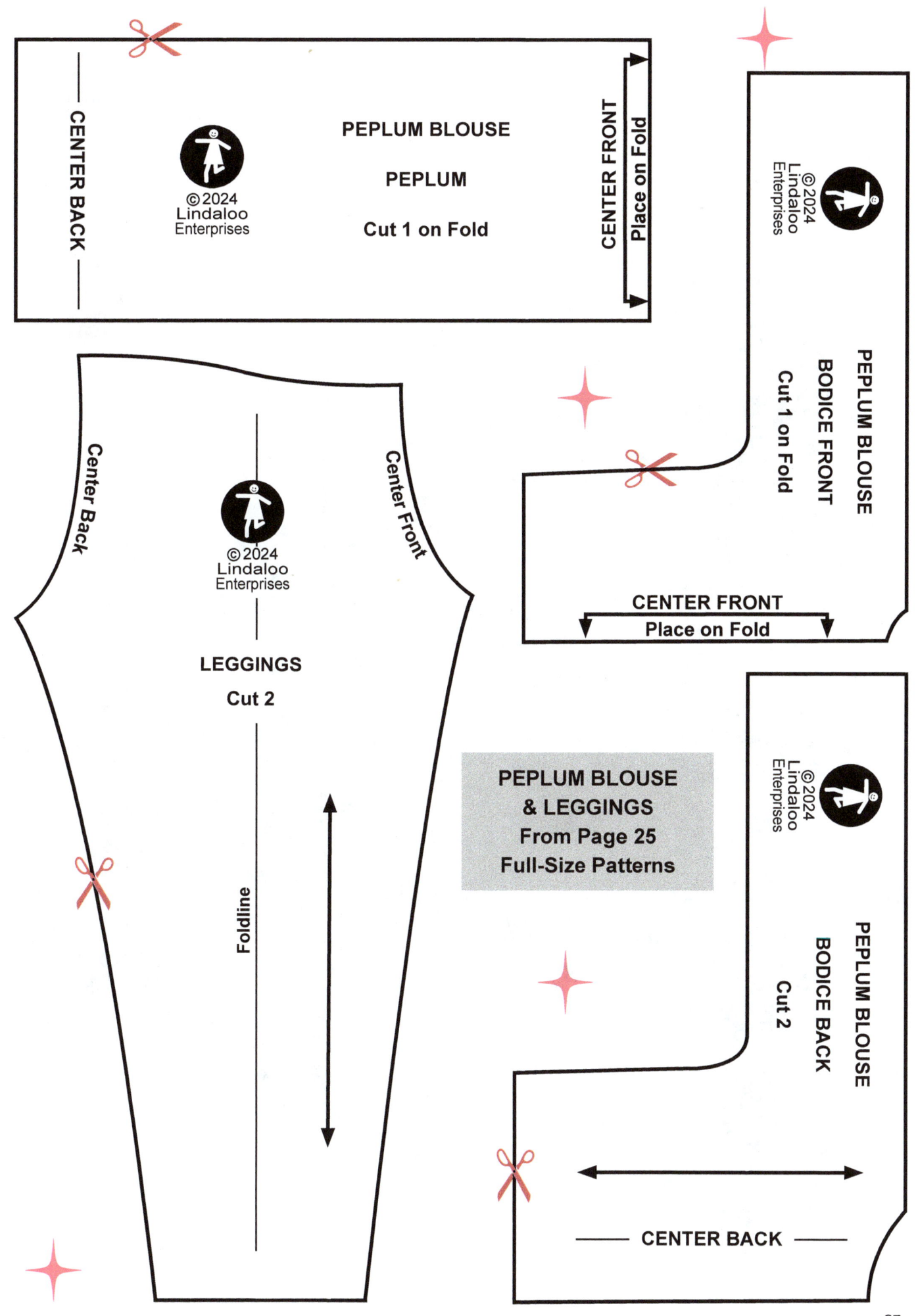

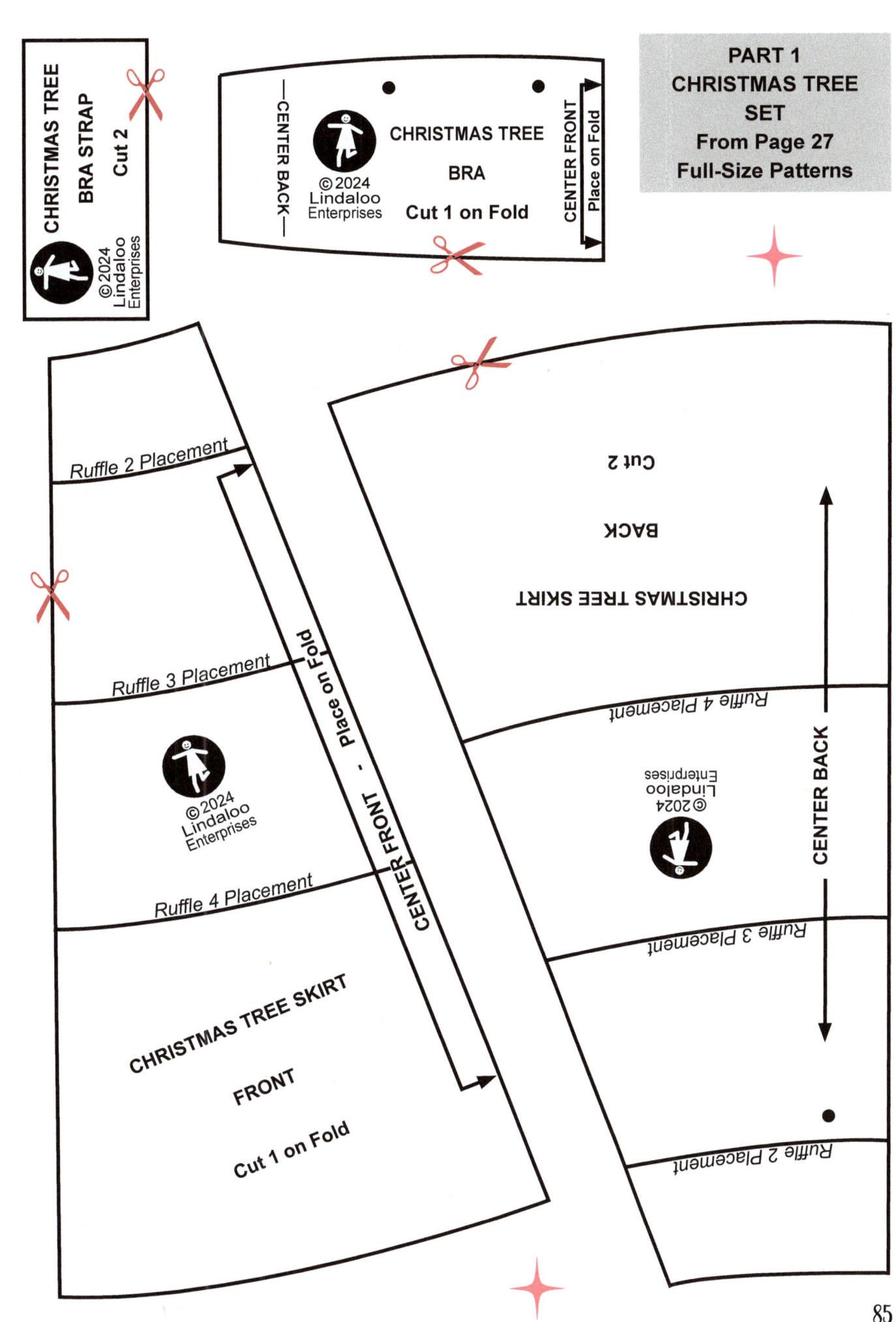

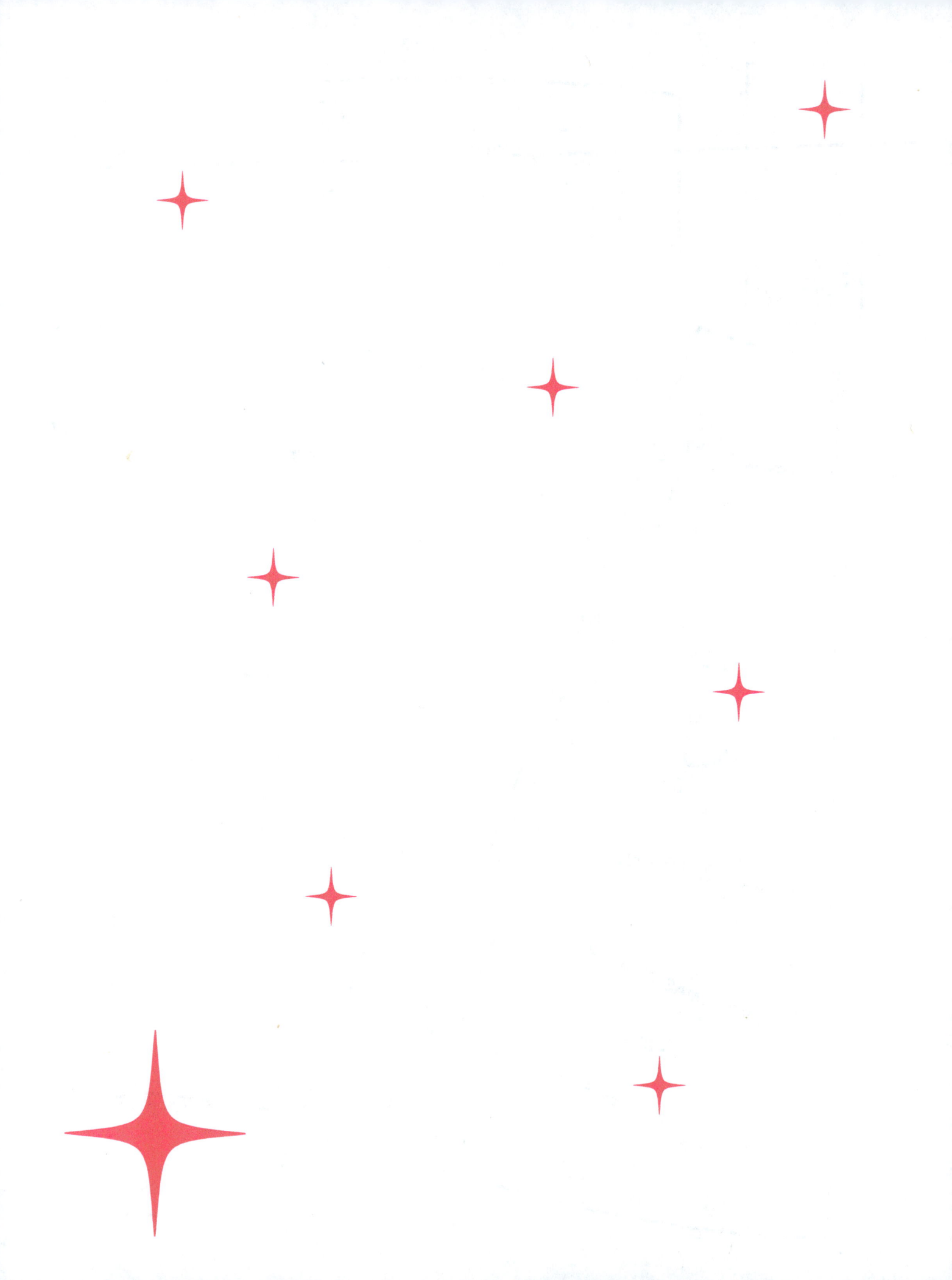

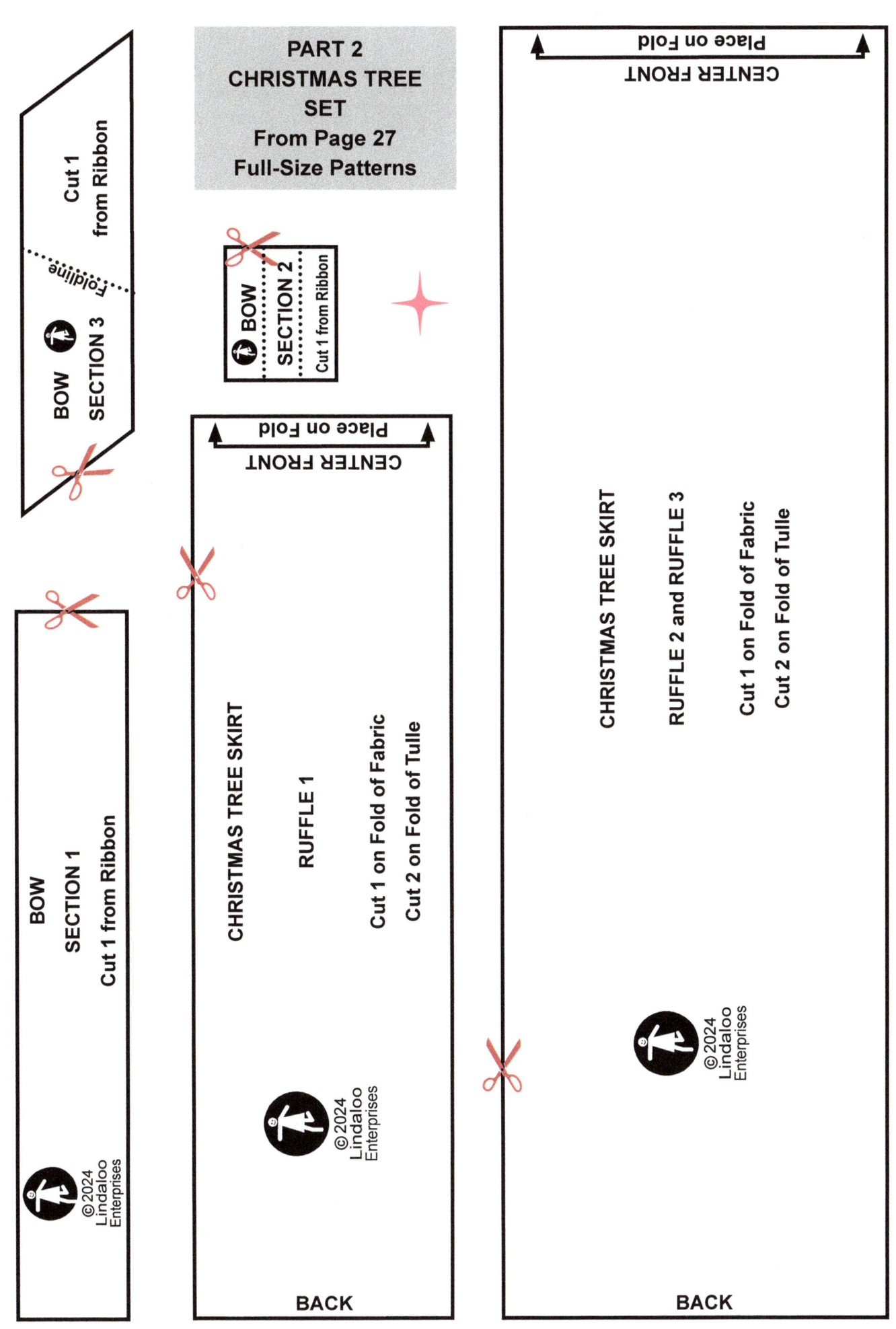

CHRISTMAS TREE SKIRT

WAISTBAND

Cut 1

**PART 3
CHRISTMAS TREE SET
From Page 27
Full-Size Patterns**

Pattern for **Ruffle 4** is in 2 sections. Tape Part A to Part B before cutting fabric & tulle.

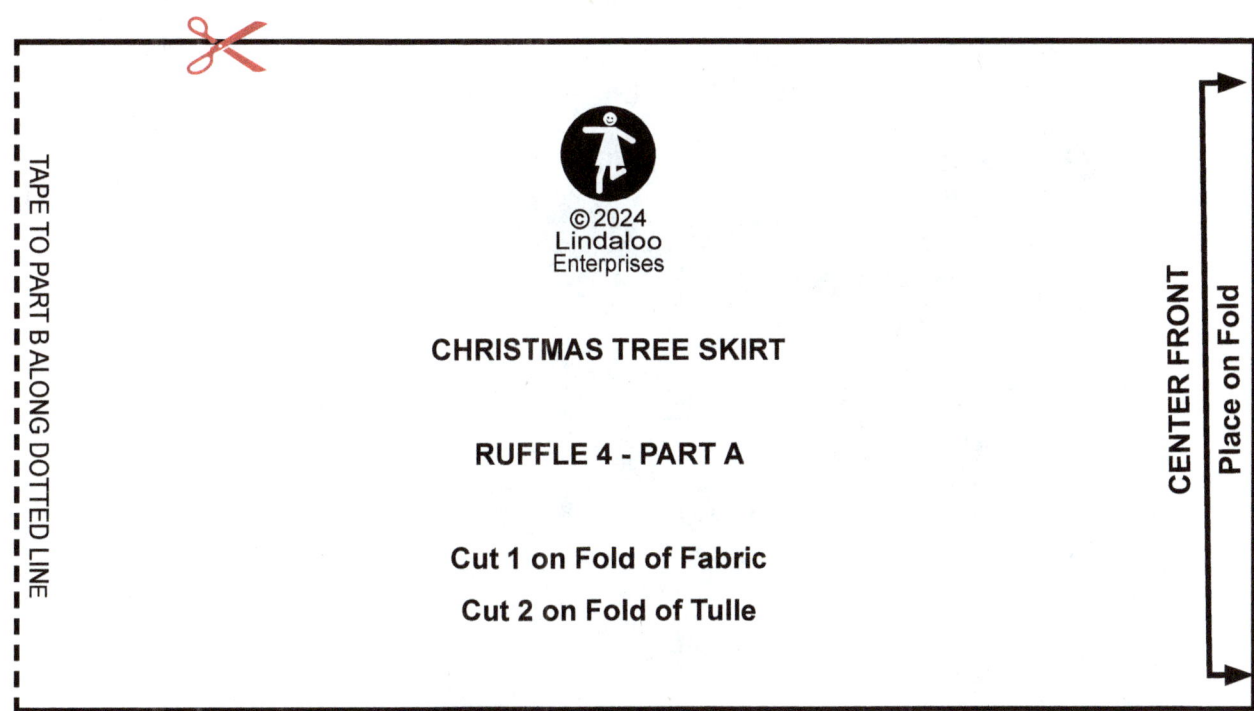

TAPE TO PART B ALONG DOTTED LINE

CHRISTMAS TREE SKIRT

RUFFLE 4 - PART A

Cut 1 on Fold of Fabric
Cut 2 on Fold of Tulle

CENTER FRONT — Place on Fold

BACK

CHRISTMAS TREE SKIRT

RUFFLE 4 - PART B

TAPE TO PART A ALONG DOTTED LINE

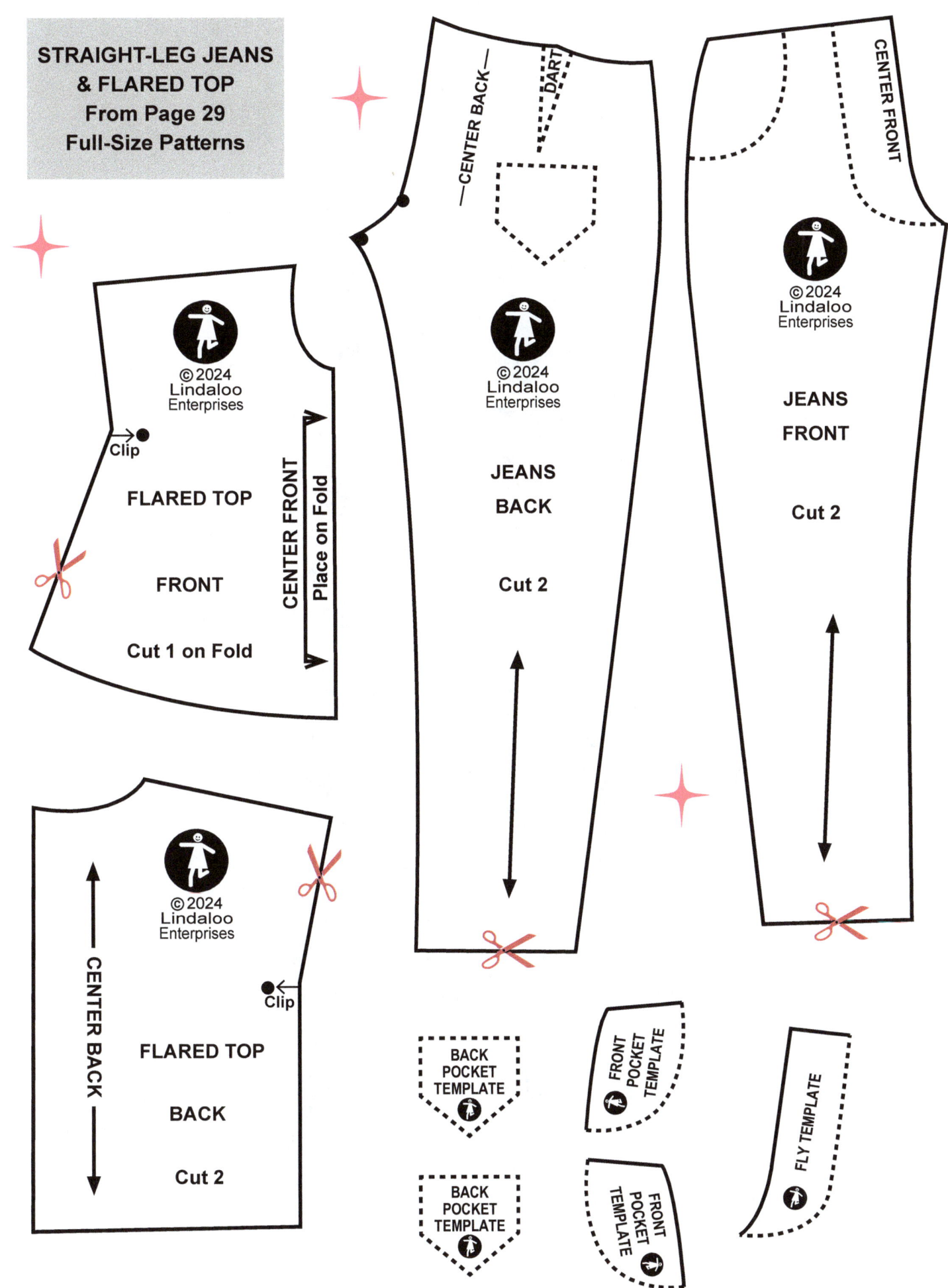

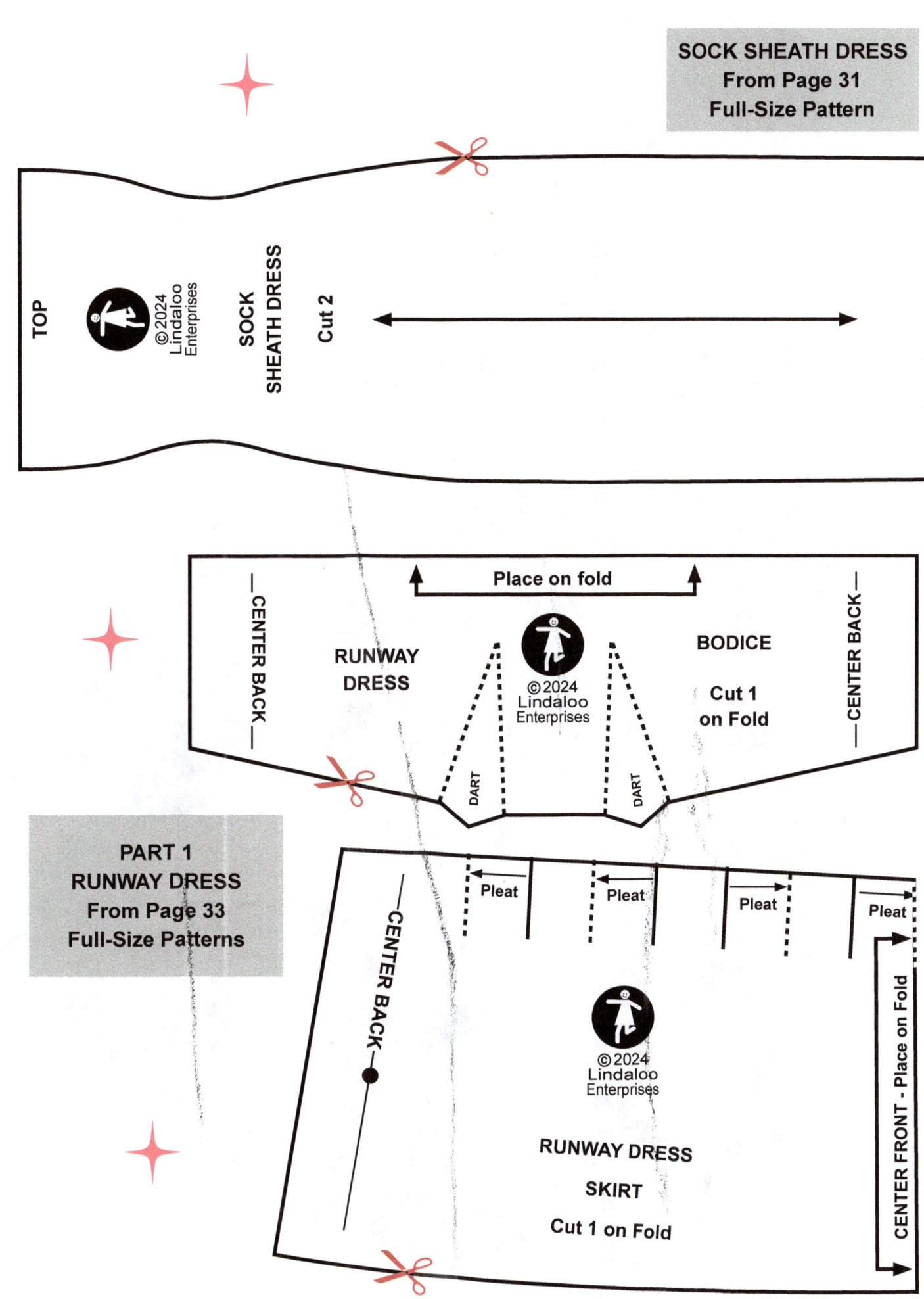

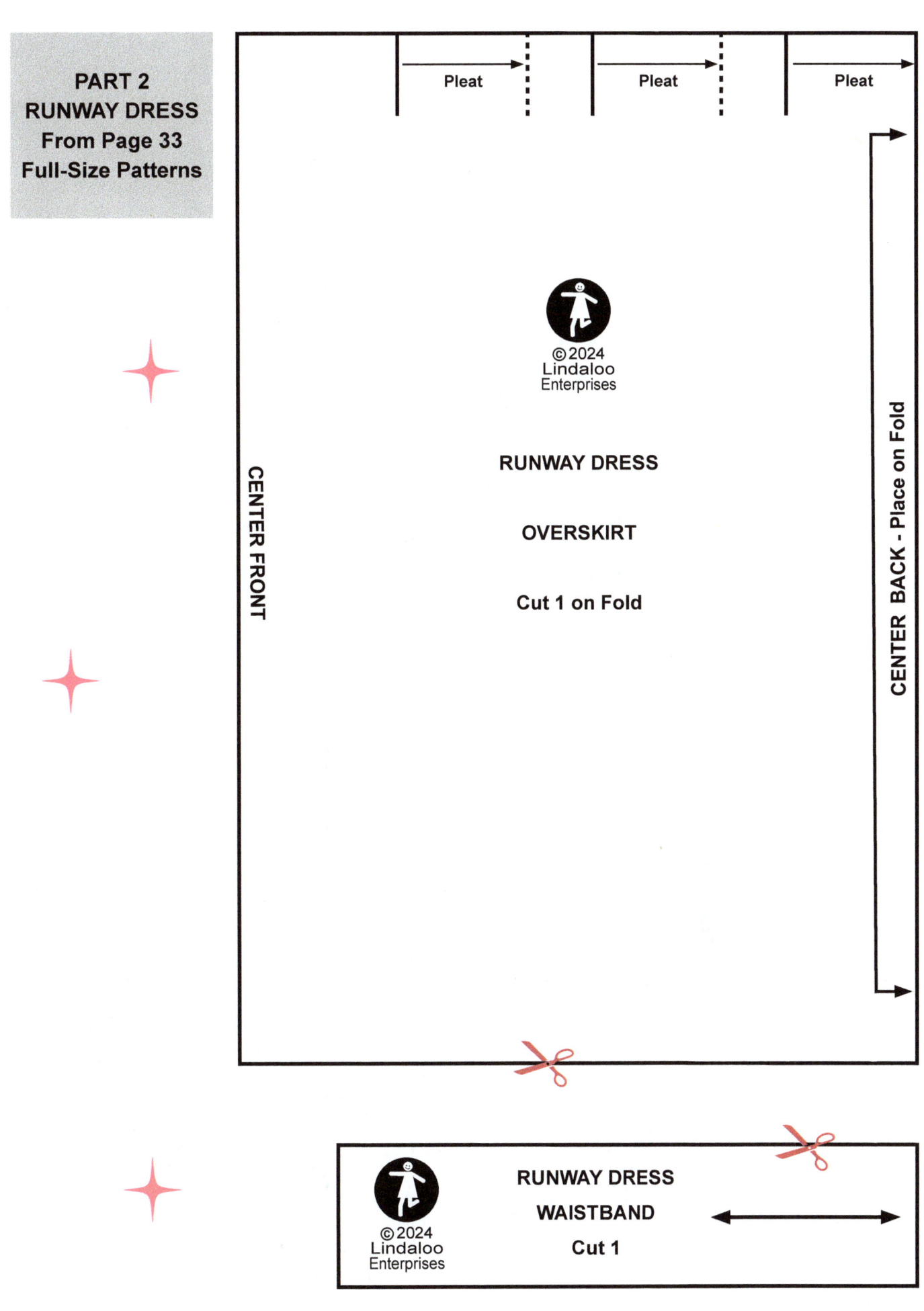

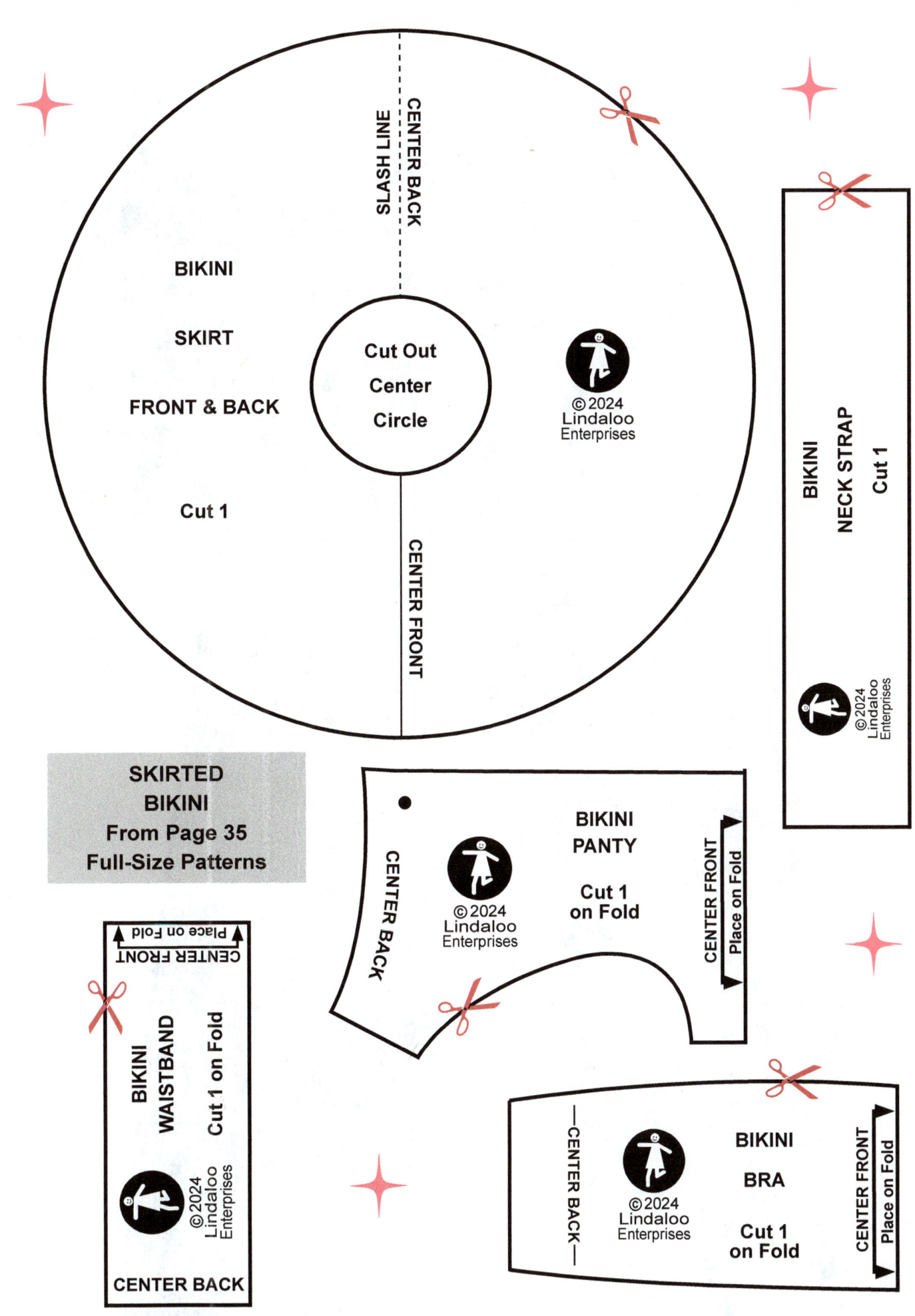

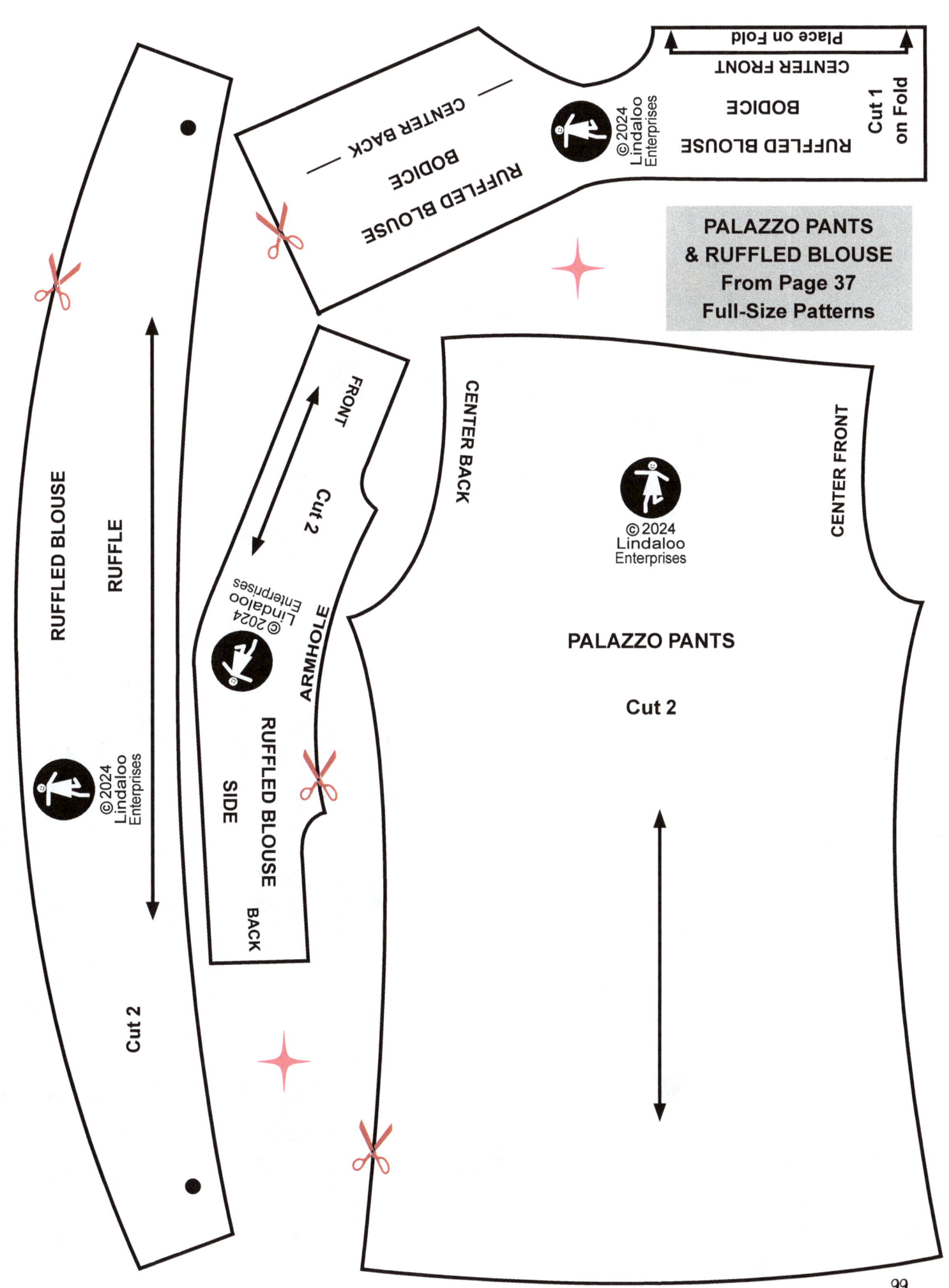

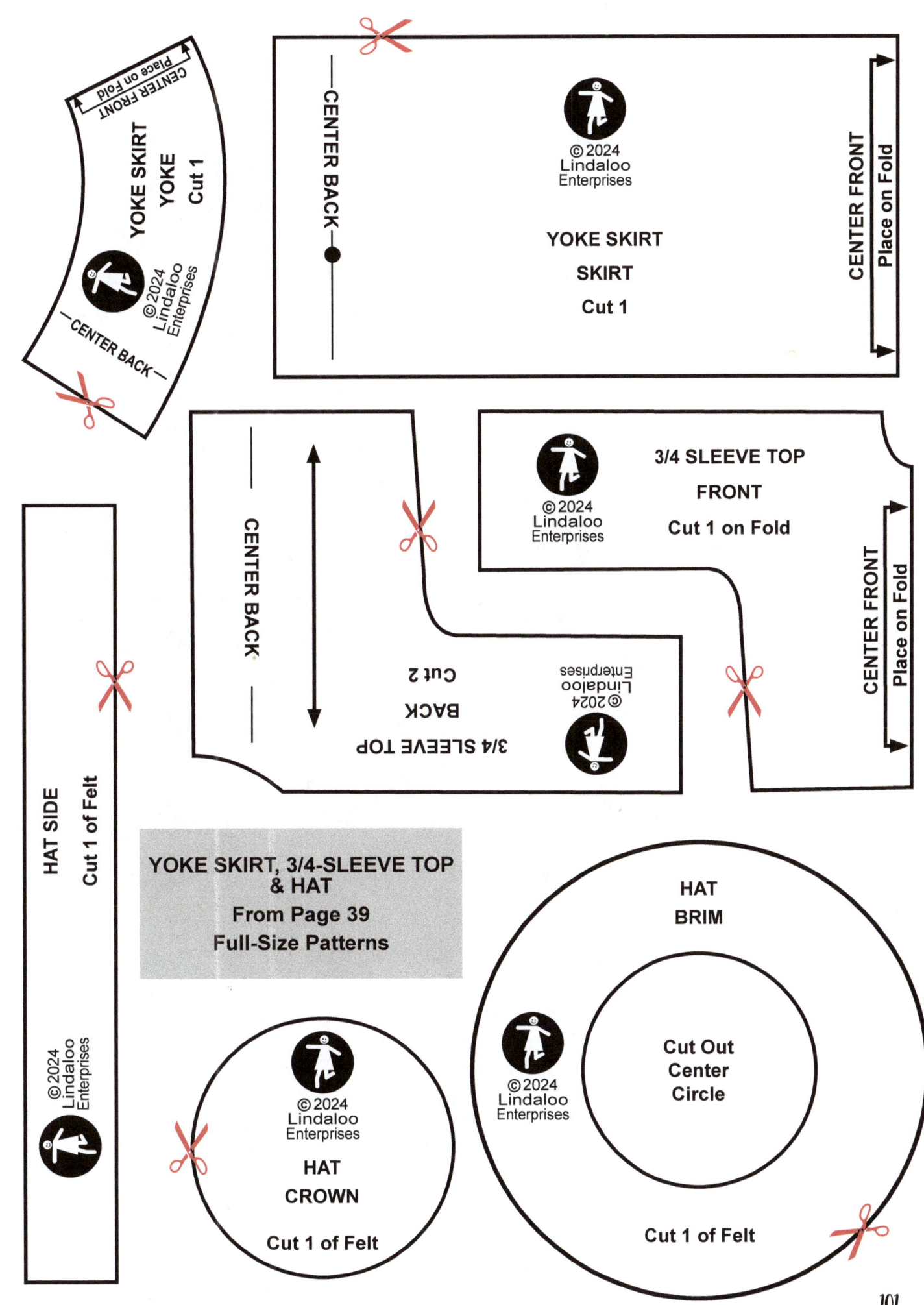

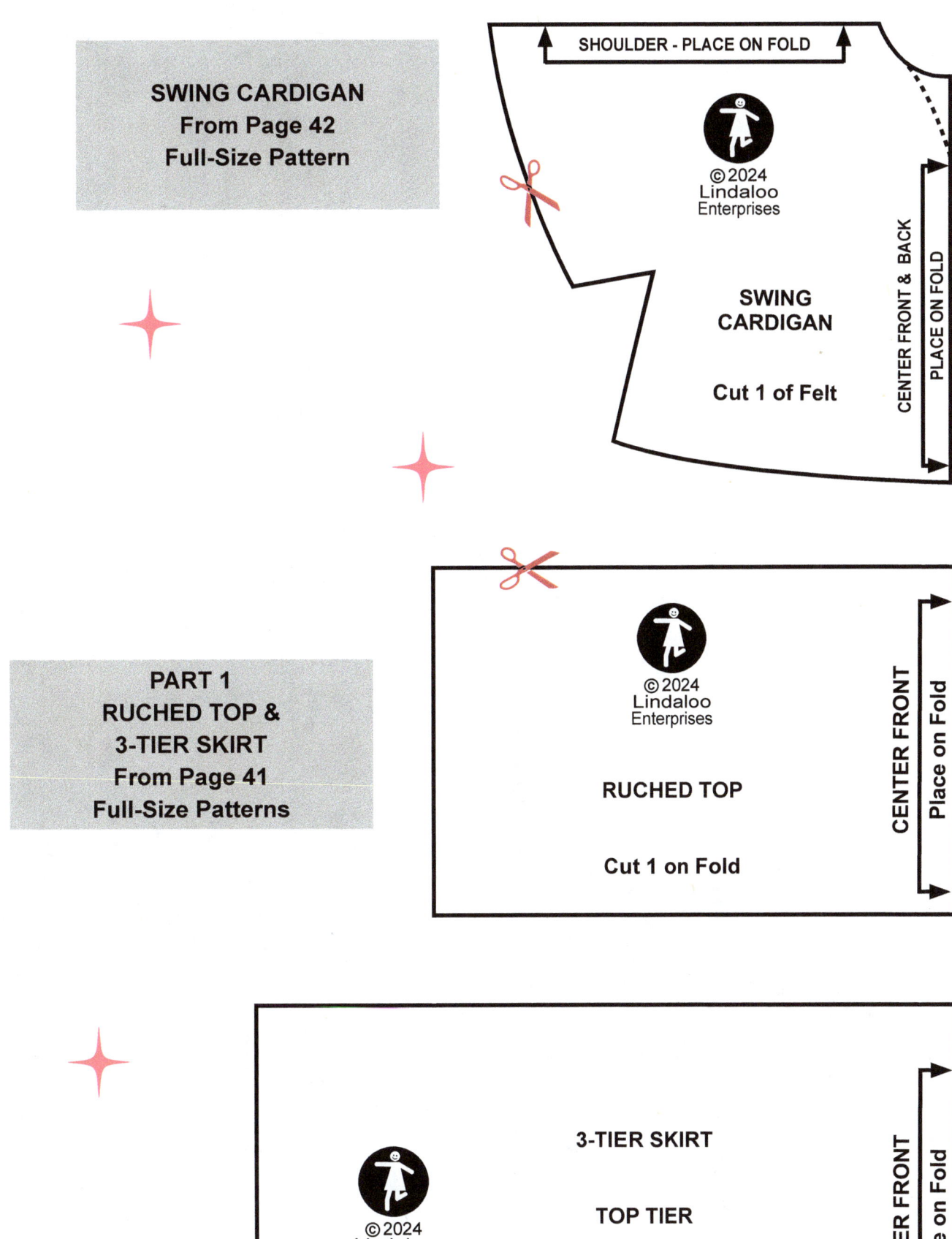

PART 2   RUCHED TOP & 3-TIER SKIRT   From Page 41   Full-Size Patterns

↑ Place on Fold ↑
CENTER FRONT

3-TIER SKIRT

MIDDLE TIER

Cut 1 on Fold

© 2024 Lindaloo Enterprises

Place on Fold

↑ Place on Fold ↑

3-TIER SKIRT

BOTTOM TIER - Part A

Cut 1 on Fold

© 2024 Lindaloo Enterprises

3-TIER SKIRT

BOTTOM TIER - Part B

Cut 1

© 2024 Lindaloo Enterprises

POM POM DRESS
From Page 45
Full-Size Patterns

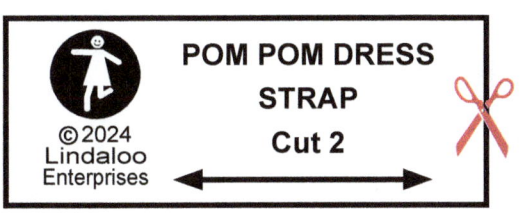

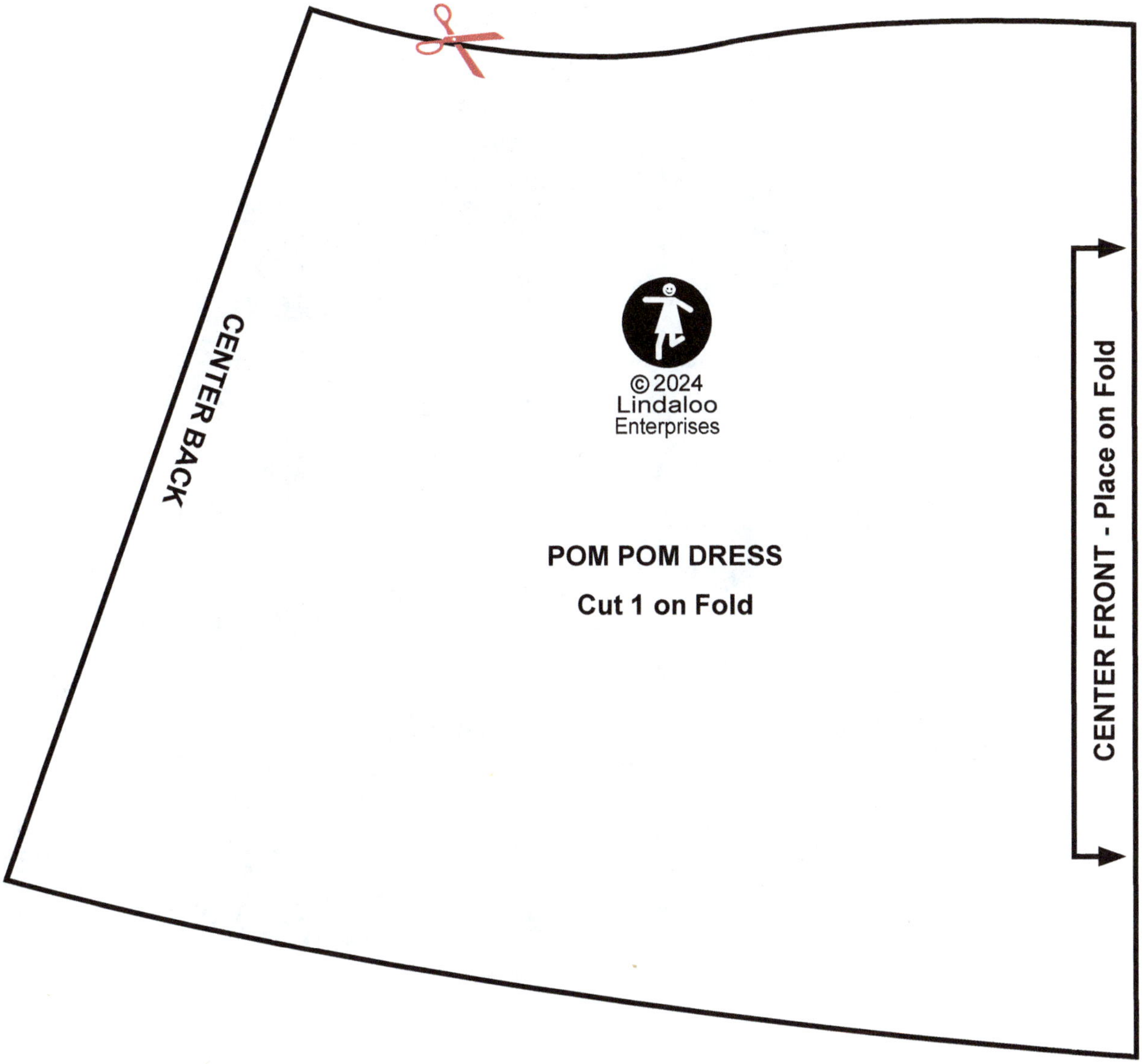

107

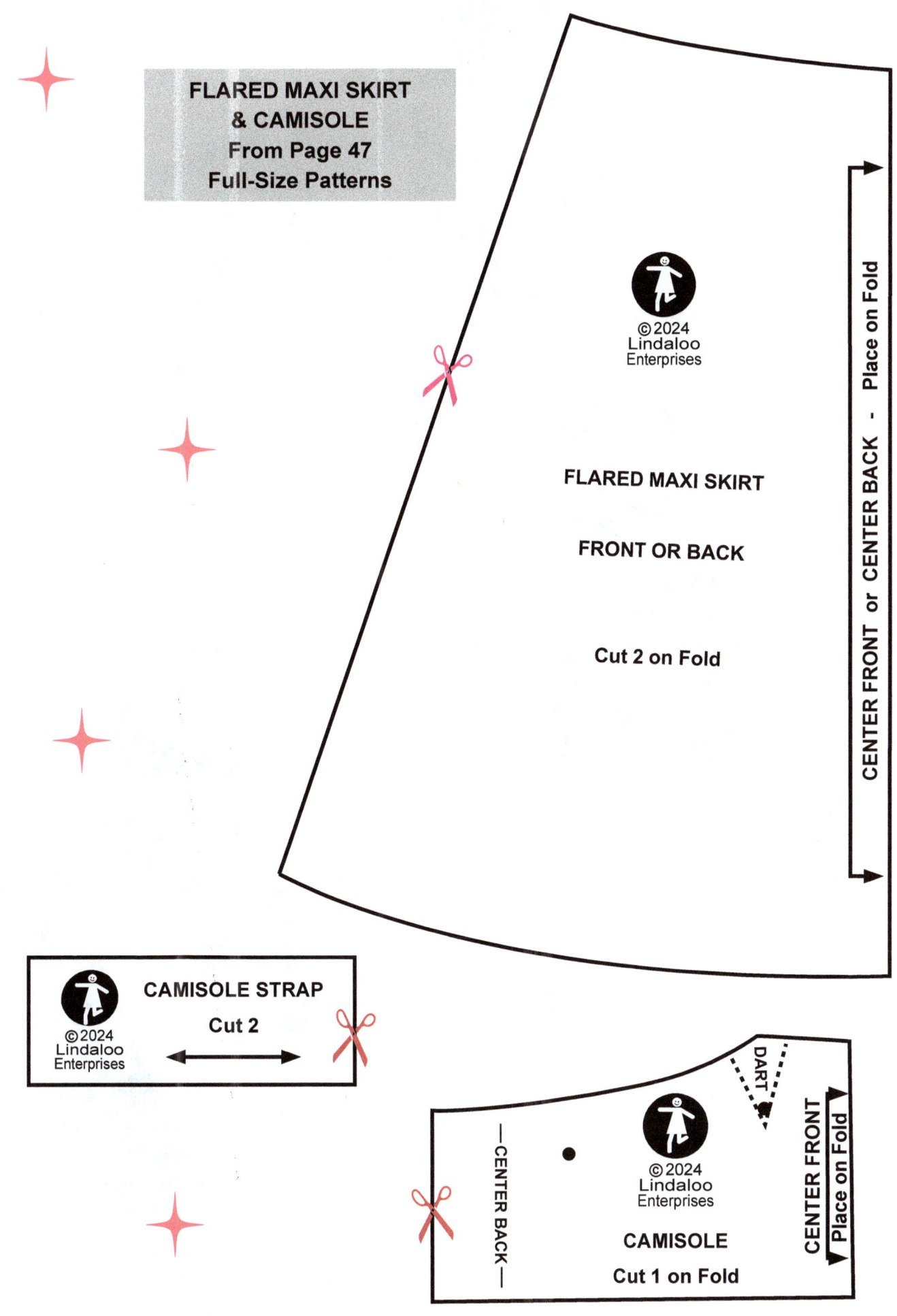

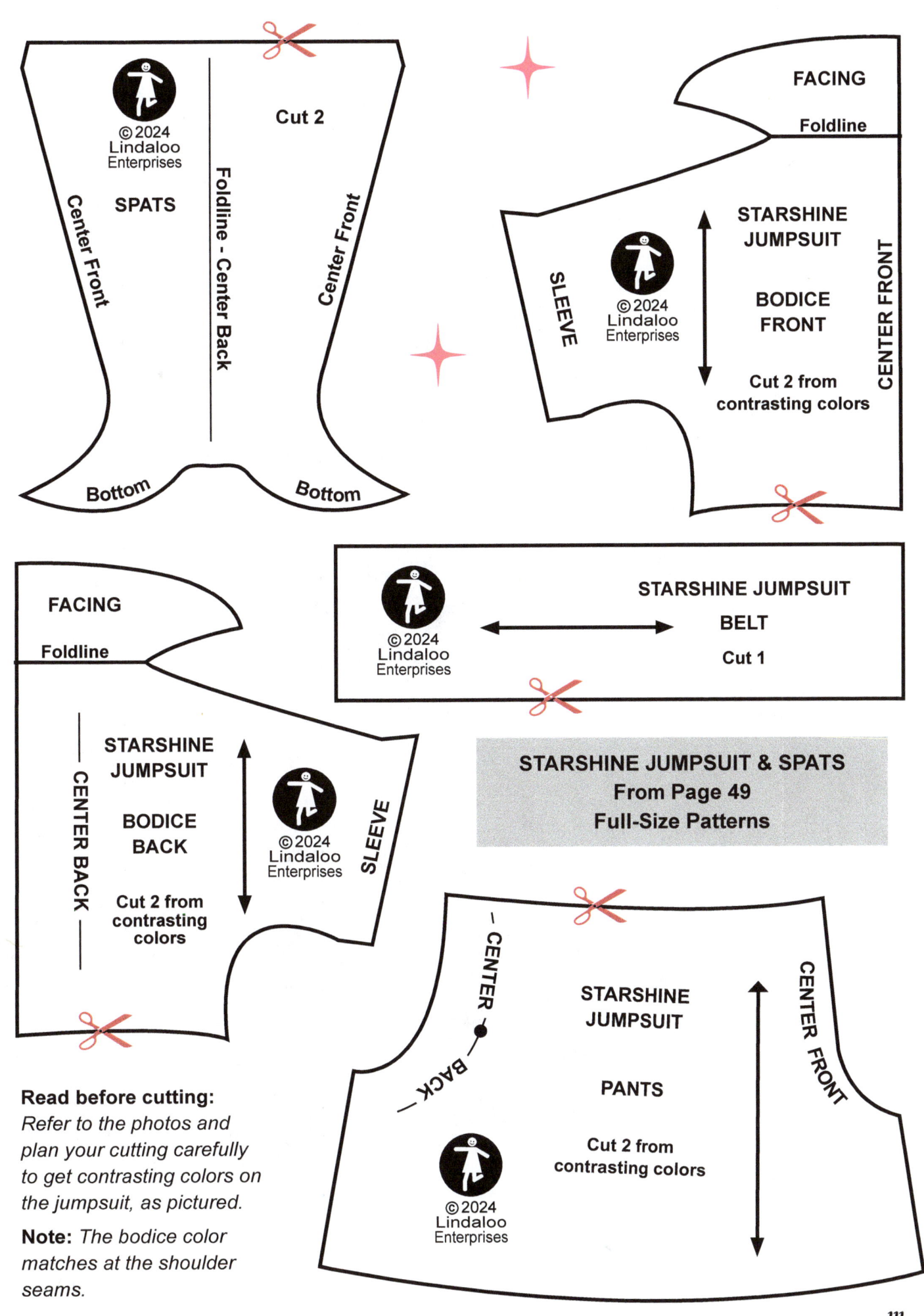

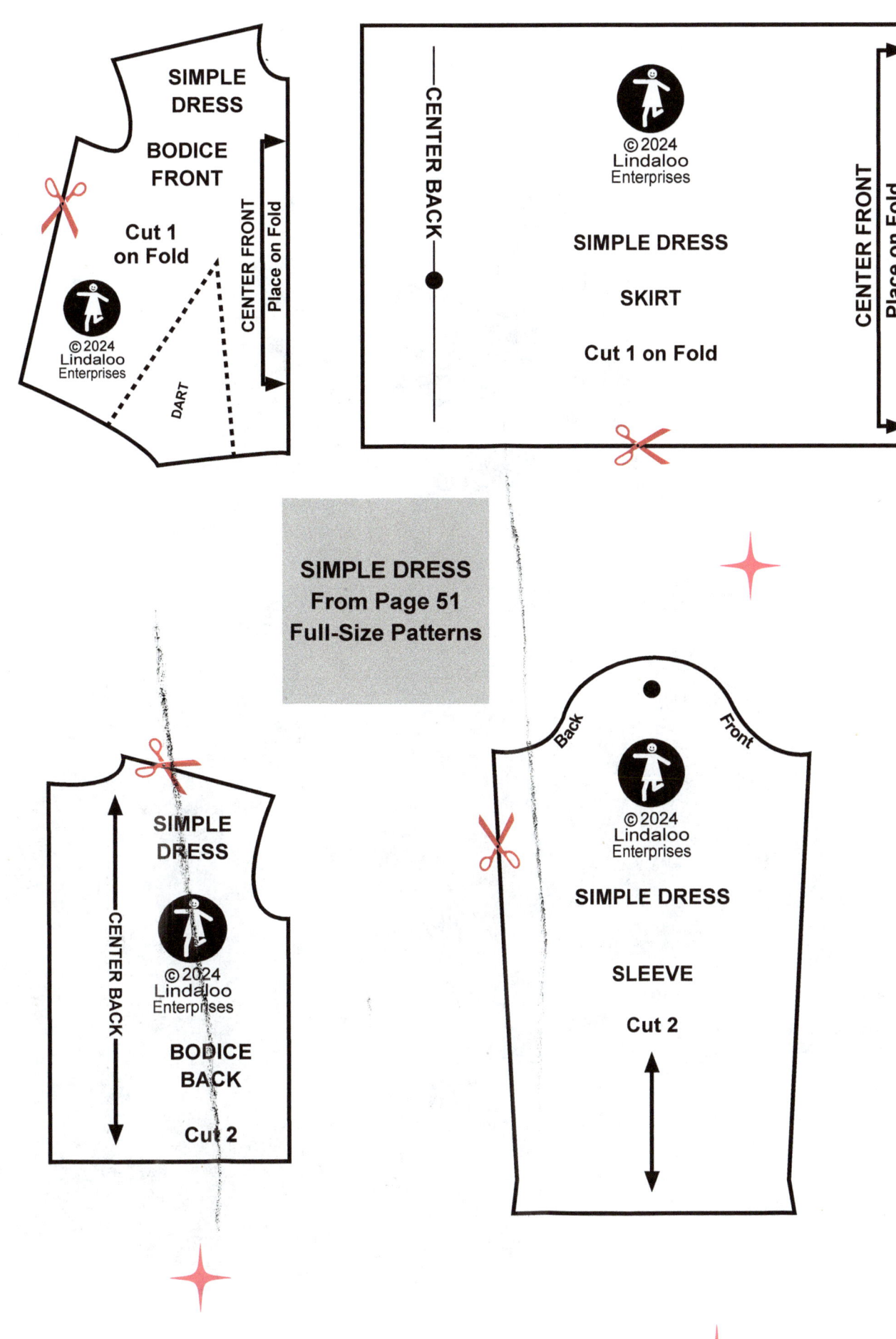

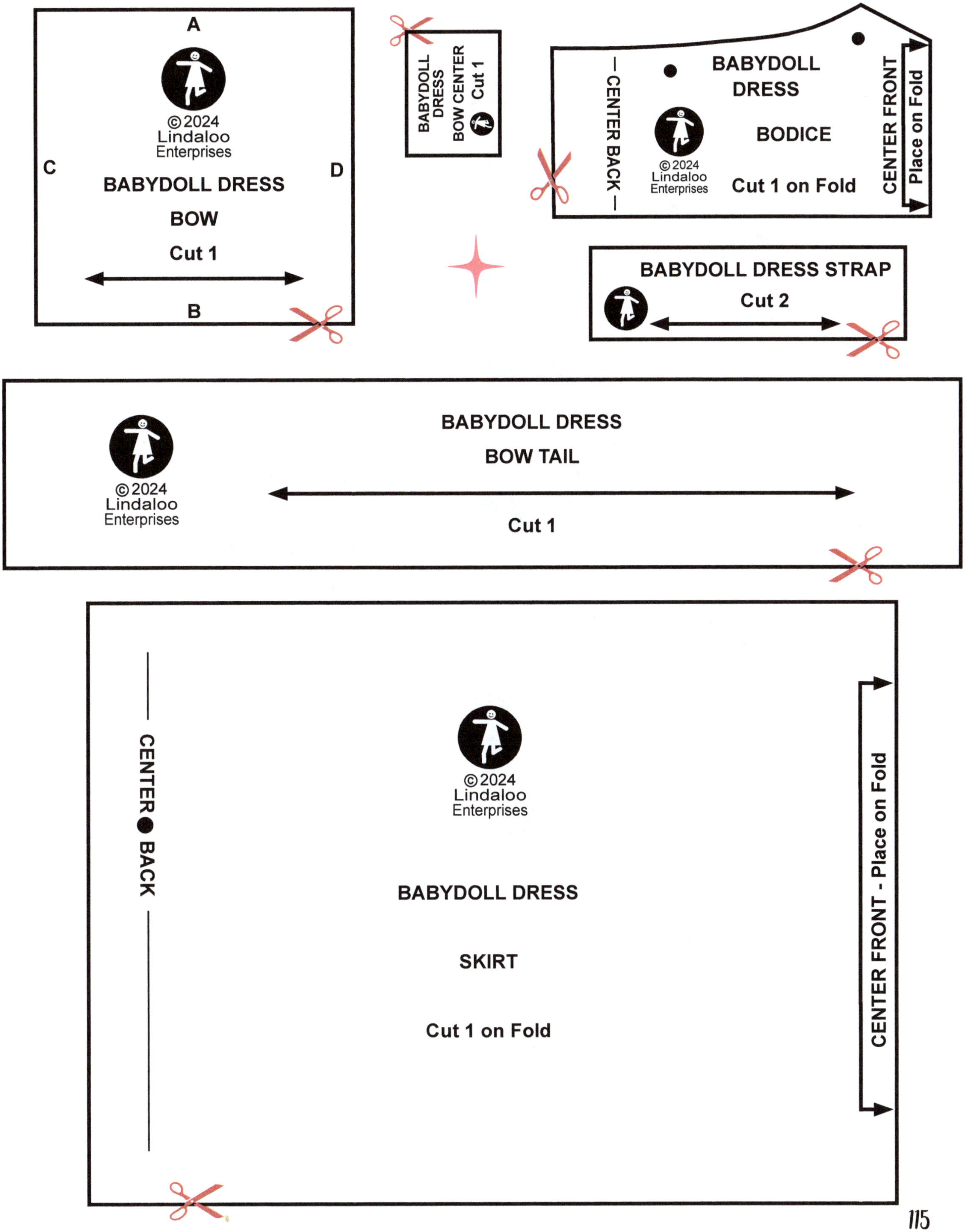

BABYDOLL DRESS From Page 53 Full-Size Patterns

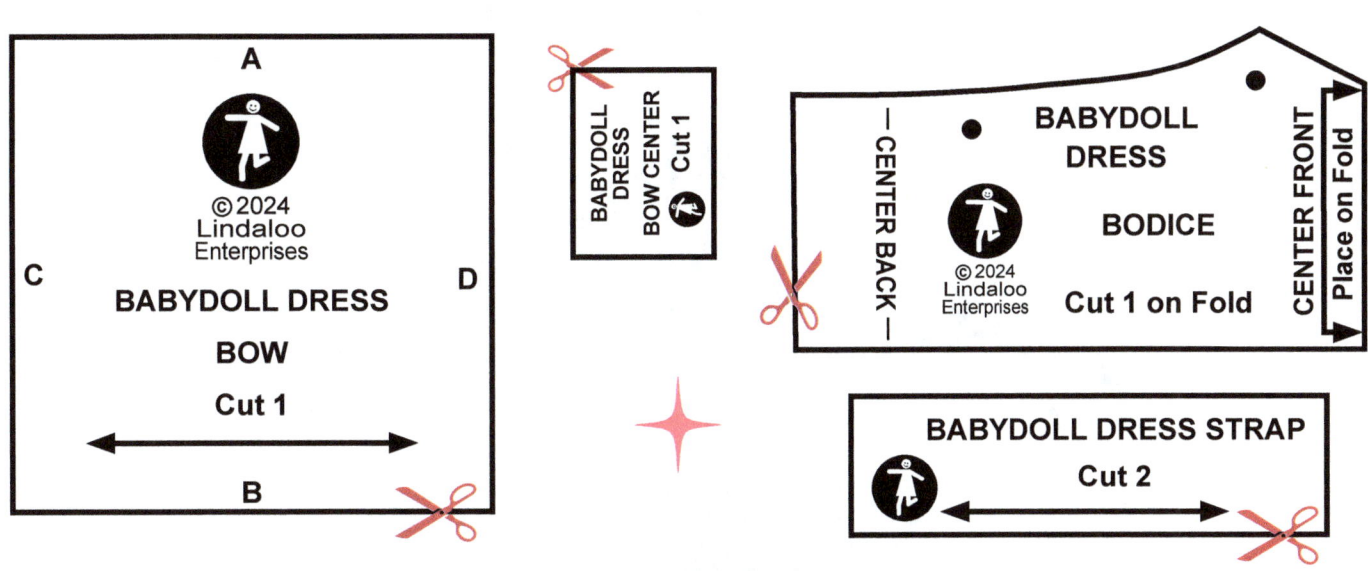

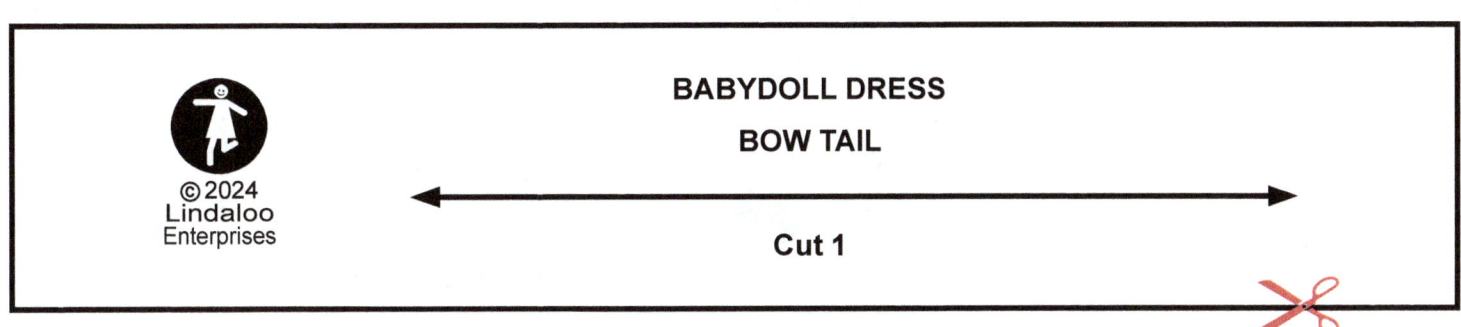

BABYDOLL DRESS

SKIRT

Cut 1 on Fold

CENTER ● BACK

CENTER FRONT - Place on Fold

NIGHTGOWN
From Page 55
Full-Size Patterns

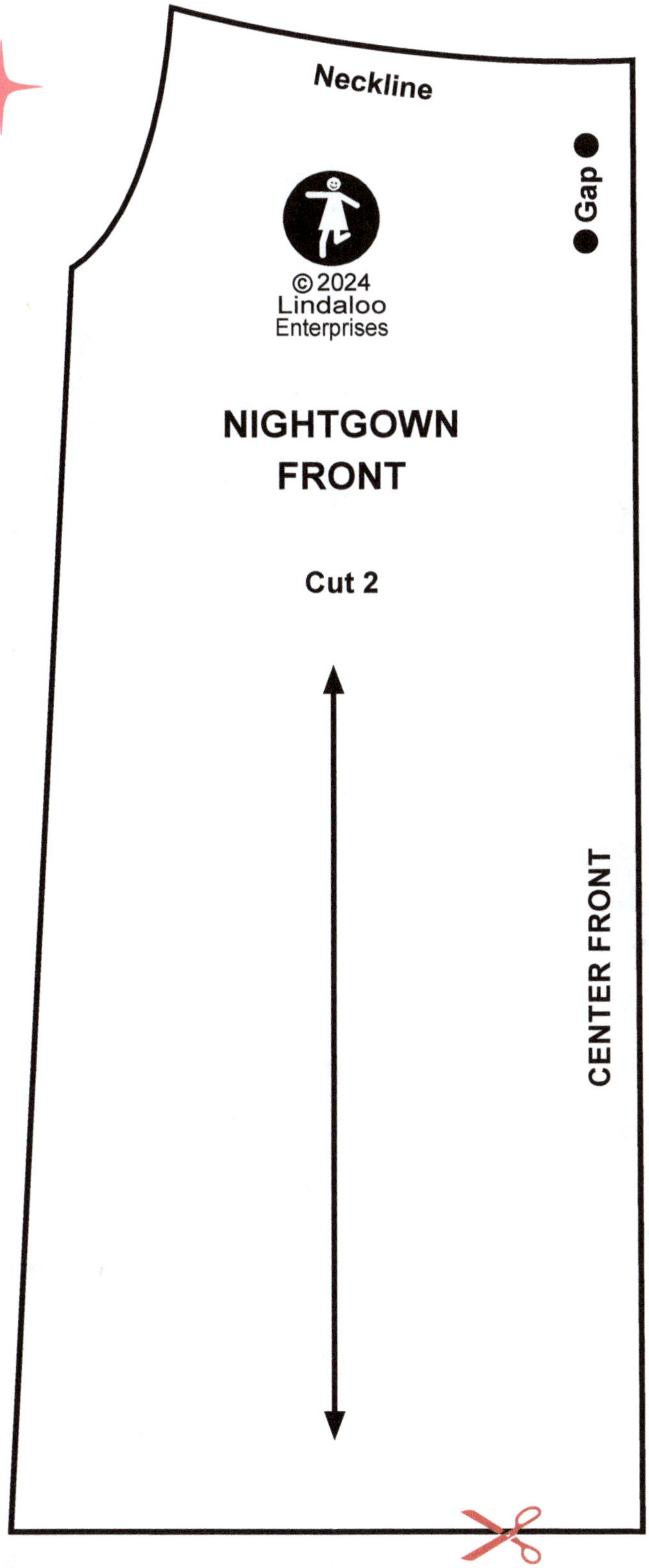

BATHROBE   From Page 55   Full-Size Pattern

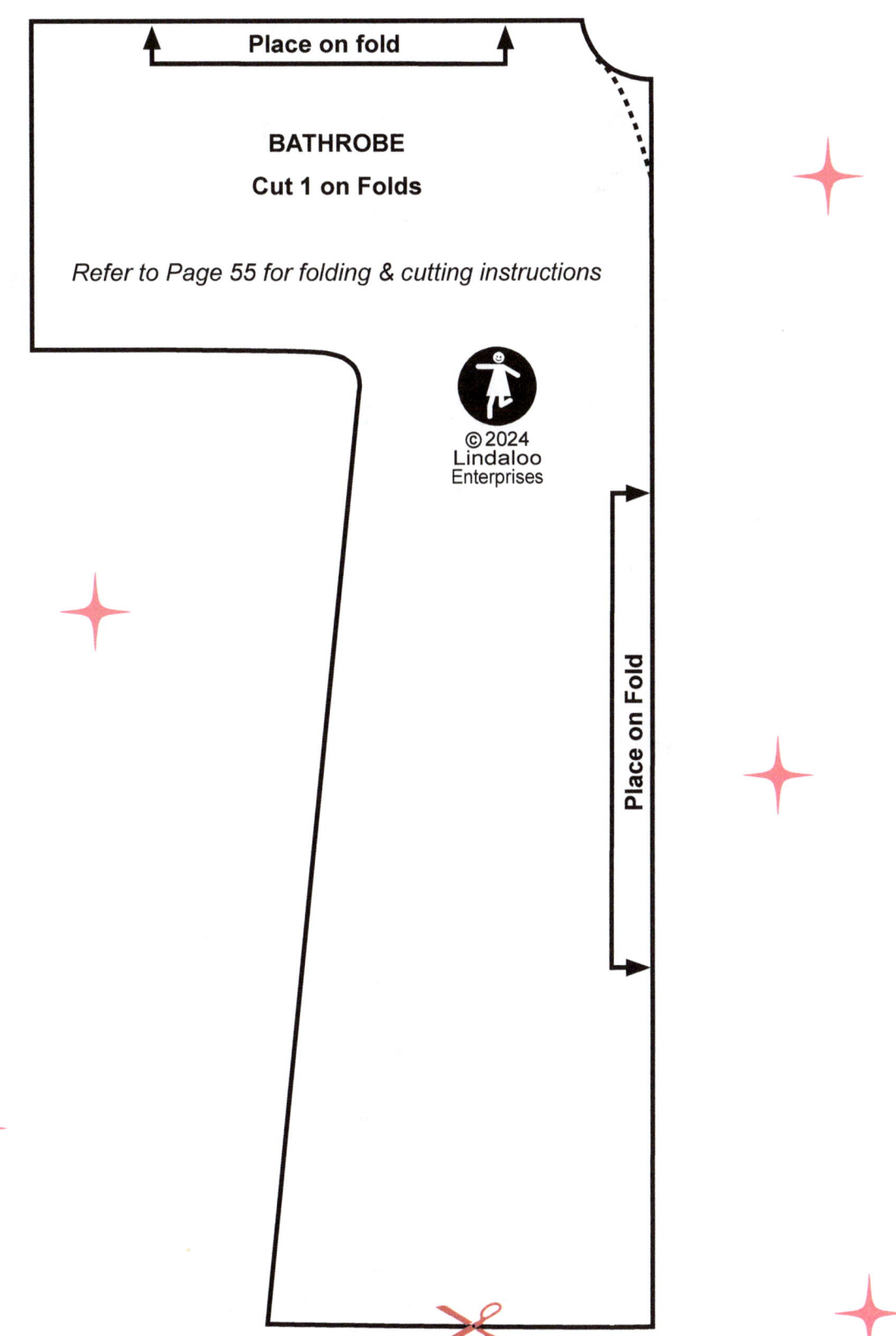

HOSIERY   From Pages 56-57   Full-Size Patterns

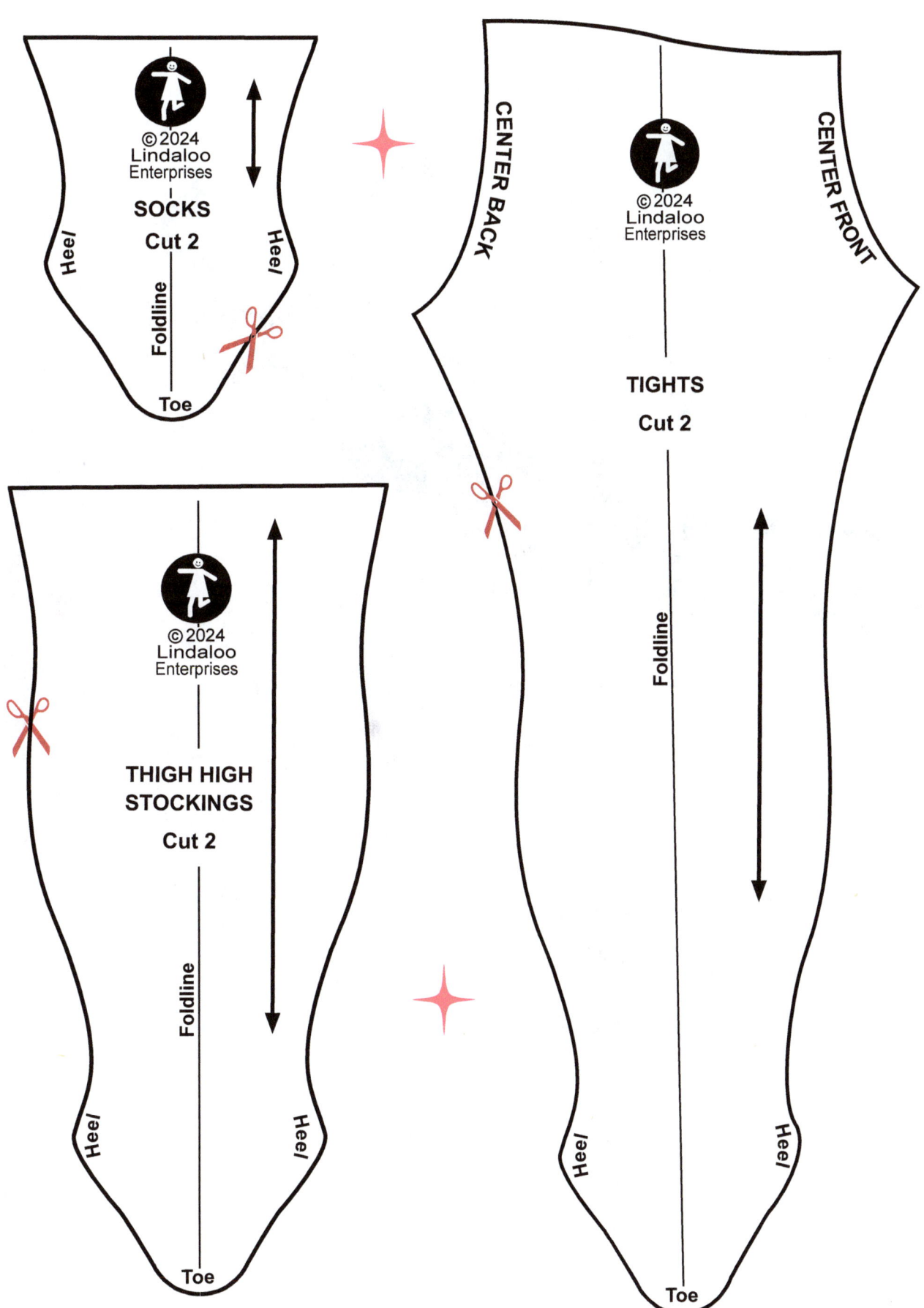

121

APRON
From Page 58
Full-Size Patterns

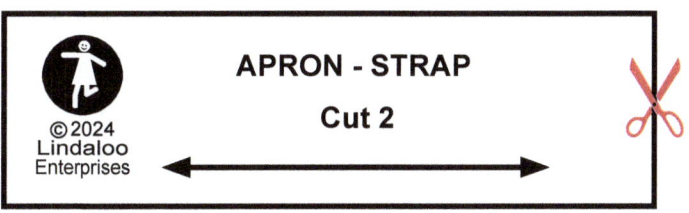

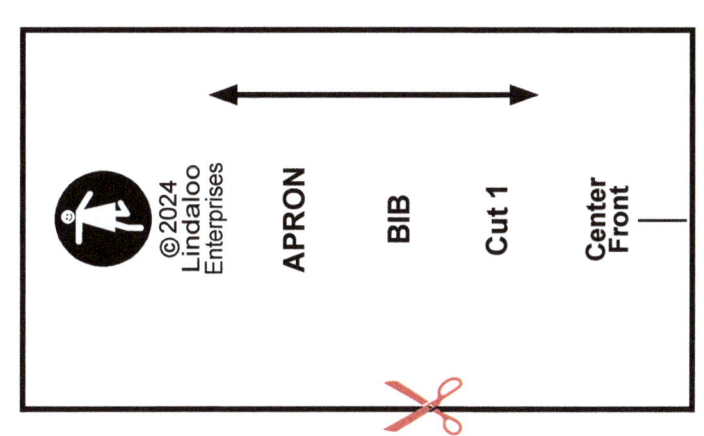

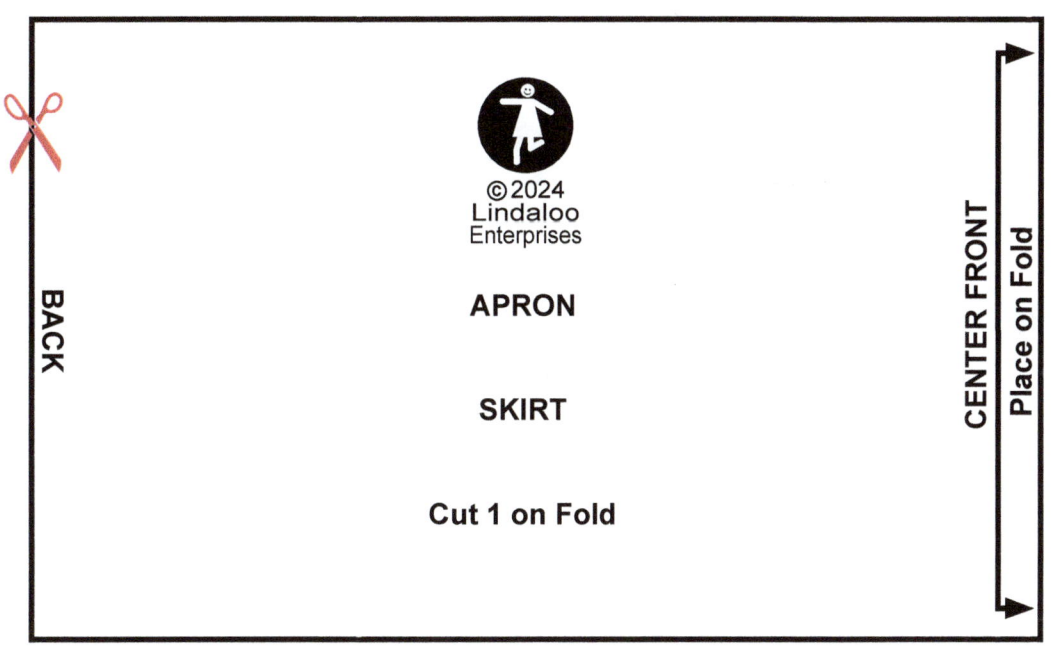

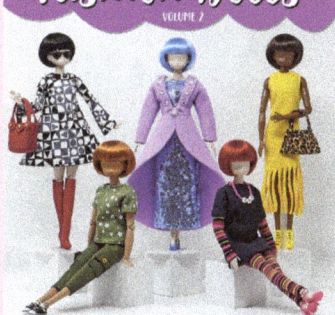

About the Author

LINDA WRIGHT studied textiles, patternmaking and clothing design at the Pennsylvania State University and has had a lifelong love of creating. She is the author of assorted handicraft books including doll clothes sewing patterns, amigurumi-style crochet, coloring books for grown-ups and her groundbreaking *Toilet Paper Origami*.

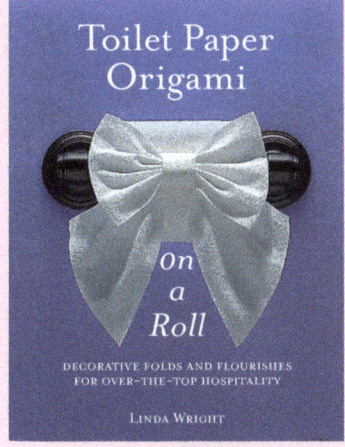
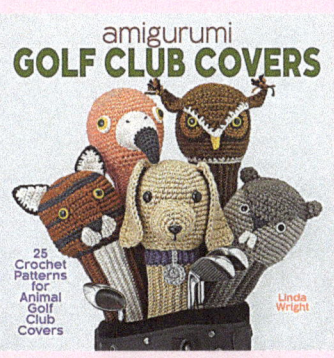
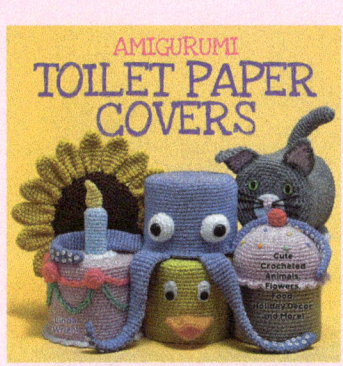

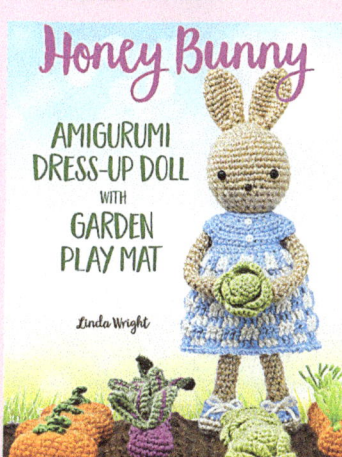
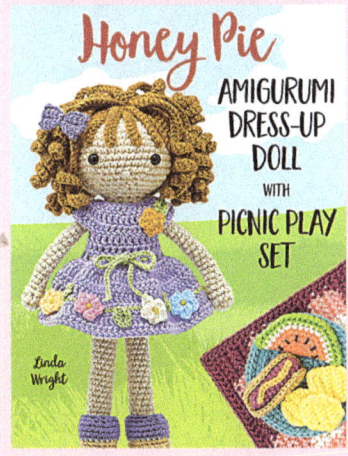
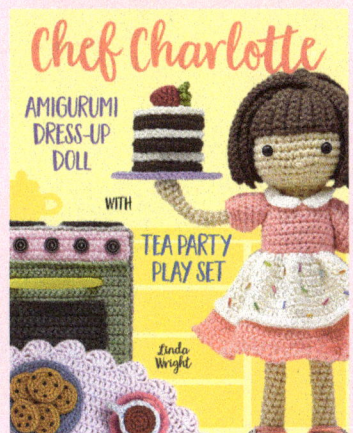

amazon.com/author/lindawright   pinterest.com/LindalooEnt   tiktok.com/@lindaloo_enterprises

www.ingramcontent.com/pod-product-compliance
Lightning Source LLC
Chambersburg PA
CBHW062132160426
43191CB00013B/2273